WAL★MART
the high cost of low price

Greg Spotts

disinformation®

Cover image: Daniel Morduchowicz
Back cover photo: Tom Bocse (Creative Commons – some rights reserved)
Layout: Maya Shmuter

Published by The Disinformation Company Ltd.
163 Third Avenue, Suite 108
New York, NY 10003
Tel.: +1.212.691.1605
Fax: +1.212.691.1606
www.disinfo.com

Library of Congress Control Number: 2005934141

ISBN-13: 978-1-932857-24-5
ISBN-10: 1-932857-24-9

Printed in USA

10 9 8 7 6 5 4 3 2 1

Distributed in the USA and Canada by:
Consortium Book Sales and Distribution
1045 Westgate Drive, Suite 90
St Paul, MN 55114
Toll Free: +1.800.283.3572 Local: +1.651.221.9035 Fax: +1.651.221.0124
www.cbsd.com

Distributed in the United Kingdom and Eire by:
Virgin Books
Thames Wharf Studios, Rainville Road
London W6 9HA
Tel.: +44.(0)20.7386.3300 Fax: +44.(0)20.7386.3360
E-Mail: sales@virgin-books.co.uk

Distributed in Australia by:
Tower Books
Unit 2/17 Rodborough Road
Frenchs Forest NSW 2086
Tel.: +61.2.9975.5566 Fax: +61.2.9975.5599
E-mail: towerbks@zip.com.au

Attention colleges and universities, unions and other organizations:
Quantity discounts are available on bulk purchases of this book for educational training purposes, fund-raising, or gift giving. Special books, booklets, or book excerpts can also be created to fit your specific needs. For information contact Marketing Department of The Disinformation Company Ltd.

WAL★MART
the high cost of low price

Contents

Foreword

The Inside Story

Filmmaker's Toolbox

About the Filmmaker

Robert Greenwald is the director/producer of *Outfoxed: Rupert Murdoch's War on Journalism* (2004), a documentary exposing the right-wing bias of Fox News. The film was initially distributed solely on DVD, but strong viewer demand led to an unusual post-DVD theatrical release in the summer of 2004.

Greenwald is also the executive producer of a trilogy of "Un" documentaries: *Unprecedented: The 2000 Presidential Election* (2002), directed by Richard Ray Perez and Joan Sekler; *Uncovered: The Whole Truth About the Iraq War* (2003), which Greenwald directed; and *Unconstitutional: The War on Our Civil Liberties* (2004), directed by Nonny de la Peña.

In addition to his documentary work, Greenwald has produced and/or directed more than fifty television movies, miniseries, and feature films, including *The Book of Ruth* (2004), based on the best-selling book by Jane Hamilton; *The Crooked E: The Unshredded Truth About Enron* (2003); *Blonde* (2001), a miniseries based on Joyce Carol Oates' fictionalized biography of Marilyn Monroe; *Our Guys: Outrage at Glen Ridge* (1999), based on the true story of a rape in a small town; *Forgotten Prisoners* (1990), about the work of Amnesty International; *Hiroshima: Out of the Ashes* (1990); *Shattered Spirits* (1986), about alcoholism, starring Martin Sheen; and *The Burning Bed* (1984), starring Farrah Fawcett as an abused housewife.

Greenwald also produced and directed the feature film *Steal This Movie* (2000), starring Vincent D'Onofrio as sixties radical Abbie Hoffman, as well as *Breaking Up* (1997), starring Russell Crowe and Salma Hayek.

Greenwald's films have garnered twenty-five Emmy nominations, four cable ACE Award nominations, two Golden Globe nominations, the Peabody Award, the Robert Wood Johnson Award, and eight Awards of Excellence from the Film Advisory Board. He was awarded the 2002 Producer of the Year Award by the American Film Institute. He is a co-founder (with Mike Farrell) of "Artists United," a group of actors and others opposed to the war in Iraq, which continues to work toward publicizing progressive causes.

Robert Greenwald has been the recipient of the 2003 Southern California ACLU Garden Party Award; the Los Angeles Physicians for Social Responsibility Peacemaker Award; the Office of the Americas Activist in the Trenches Award; Liberty Hill's Upton Sinclair Award; and was honored by the Los Angeles Chapter of the National Lawyers Guild in 2003 as "a producer and director who uses his talent and artistry to promote better understanding between people and advance the cause of peace, justice, and freedom."

the high cost of low price

Introduction

ROBERT GREENWALD

Robert Greenwald with the Panasonic DVX100a camera.

I am writing this at five in the morning, after almost a year of intense work on *Wal-Mart: The High Cost of Low Price*. It's very hard to have much perspective when there's so much yet to do in finishing the film and getting it out into the world, but the most difficult part is over, and since the deadline for the book has arrived, it's now or never.

Let me say, first off, that it has been an amazing ride. My colleagues at Brave New Films are a remarkable group of dedicated, fearless, and tireless workers. (More about them later.) And I want to acknowledge the Wal-Mart employees, past and present, who have inspired all of us to keep going every exhausting, difficult, and frustrating day. These workers, who punch the time clocks day-in and day-out, are real heroes. They deserve better, and that's one of the many reasons we made this film.

I went into this film knowing very little about Wal-Mart, but I came out furious, saddened, and committed to being part of the long-term effort to change the company. It has immense, global corporate influence, over jobs, sweatshops, communities, and the environment. I have been staggered at the power that Wal-Mart exerts over millions of people's daily lives, without any fingerprints!

I have made more than sixty films, but none as demanding as this one, with its unique combination of funding nightmares, a brutal time deadline, and its enormous size and scope.

Let me explain.

Funding nightmares. After going ahead with my previous documentaries *Uncovered* and *Outfoxed* without sufficient funding, relying instead on our friendly banker and loan officer, I vowed I would not do it again. It was too difficult, and created stress that only added to the already intense political and creative pressure we felt. But along came *Wal-Mart*, and not only did I go ahead with virtually no funding, but I did so with a budget that ultimately rose to $1.6 million during filming, versus the $500,000 of *Outfoxed* and the $350,000 of *Uncovered*. This was my mistake and mine alone, since everyone advised against it, and it has been a heavy price to pay in the sense of having to fundraise at the same time as making the film. I thought I had solved the problem, only to have a major source of funds pull out because of fear that Wal-Mart would blacklist him and refuse to carry his company's DVDs and videos in their stores. This was the first (but not the last) incident of serious fear affecting friends and allies whom I had hoped would help with the film.

So my friendly banker came to the rescue again, but this time for big, *big* money, and as I write I am hoping we can crawl out of the red and into the black with help from other individual funders, foundations, and DVD sales. If not, I may come knocking on your door with my family to bunk with you! (But as I write, with Hurricane Katrina wreaking havoc,

the high cost of low price

it is hard to complain or be glib.)

Brutal time deadline. With both *Uncovered* and *Outfoxed*, I had agreed to impossibly short production schedules because of the immediacy of the issues involved. My partners, Wes Boyd at MoveOn.org and John Podesta of the Center for American Progress, both wisely insisted on these deadlines for political reasons. And they were right. Both the war in Iraq and the propaganda from Fox News in the run-up to the presidential election were time-critical subjects.

With the Wal-Mart film, I wanted to avoid the all-night editing, the seven-day workweeks, and the production team's exhaustion. So I insisted on a year to make the film, which seemed generous compared to the six-to-eight month schedules of the previous films. Unfortunately, I had grossly misjudged the demands of the film.

Because I chose to pursue a different creative model (more *Hoop Dreams* than *Outfoxed*), and because of my total inexperience with this kind of documentary, I had no idea that it would take months just to find the right stories, and that it would take weeks of living with our subjects while shooting hours and hours of tape to get the footage we needed. My one-year deadline proved woefully unrealistic, especially given that we had to "lock" the picture two months in advance due to the technical requirements of getting the DVD ready. Needless to say, we have had all-night editing and endless seven-day workweeks, and the BNF group has had to work their asses off due to this second big mistake on my part.

Enormous size and scope. I had an idea that this would be a larger film, but I was also firmly committed to deeply personal stories ("More Arthur Miller then Bertolt Brecht," as I kept saying), so I really believed the scale would be manageable. Yet, little by little, our locations expanded from Florida to Arizona to Canada to China, and dozens of places in between. We shot more than 350 hours of original footage. The desire and commitment to tell the full story was a demon on my back, pushing me harder and harder to get it right, to cover all the aspects, to leave no stone unturned—and to not screw it up! The size grew at the same time that the funding evaporated and the deadline grew closer and closer. Not the ideal recipe for easy living but, as a friend says, if it was easy, there would be a relative in the job. Thanks, BNF team.

Which leads me to the story of how this team came to be. After *Outfoxed* and *Uncovered*, when the Wal-Mart project was in its earliest, formative stage, I was prescient enough to seek the advice of Rick Jacobs. I had gotten to know Rick when he was running the Howard Dean campaign in California. He had come up with the single balls-iest idea I had heard during the heat of the primary wars. He called me out of the blue to suggest we screen *Uncovered*, not as a fundraiser for Dean, but as a collective screening for all the Democratic candidates, as a way to say to the world, we have more in common than we have dividing us. Brilliant.

Rick started talking to me about infrastructure. Not the physical infrastructure of bridges and highways, but the need for an organizing and communication infrastructure among progressives—one in which the films, videos, and short pieces I was doing could serve an important function. I was excited about the idea of a company that would tell stories that weren't getting told in the mainstream media. I consulted with my close friend and adviser Marge Tabankin, who agreed that this made sense, and that yes, I should give it a shot. While I personally had chosen to volunteer my time and skills thus far for the political films, inspired by Joan Blades and Wes Boyd of MoveOn, many of the other guerilla filmmakers needed a regular salary, however paltry. And so the company that would become Brave New Films was conceived.

I had worked with Jim Gilliam and Devin Smith on *Out-*

foxed and *Uncovered*, and I knew I had to recruit them for the new company. Jim's brilliance in all things internet-connected, plus his quick absorption of the realities of the film universe, made him invaluable. I have learned a great deal from Jim, not only about the technical part (prior to his tutoring I'd been impressed just to "reply to all"), but about the concepts behind the use of websites and blogs—the best way today to connect, engage, and converse with people. Devin had arrived at RGP, my film production company, as an unpaid intern from the American Film Institute about four years previously, working his way up from intern to assistant to producer. He came aboard to run the production and business side of Brave New Films.

I had known and worked with Lisa Smithline through her involvement with the Office of the Americas, an excellent progressive non-profit based in Los Angeles. She cheerfully and matter-of-factly got things done and returned phone calls quickly, and was even faster replying to e-mail than I was. When she became available, even without Brave New Films yet in place, I said yes, let's work together and we'll figure out what that means as time goes on. Not surprisingly, she quickly became indispensable to the BNF team.

The addition of Sarah Feeley to our team was pure luck—or magic. We had undertaken the Wal-Mart film while fully understaffed, fully under-financed, and fully under-organized. I hired Sarah for three weeks to help us with the particularly challenging task of filming fifty store openings, all on the same day at various places around the country—with no budget. Lo and behold, spreadsheets, charts, and color-coded lists appeared overnight. In no time at all, Sarah had created tool kits, field guides, and detailed instructions for our camera teams across the country. We were off and running, and Sarah's three weeks were indefinitely extended.

So we all moved forward together with a new company,

a new film, no money, and lots of ideas and enthusiasm. As we were shooting and beginning to edit the Wal-Mart film, I found that we were not only forming a powerful team, but building a brand, Brave New Films, with a product, *Wal-Mart*. (I know, I hate giving Wal-Mart any credit, but I can't find a better way to explain it.)

As I thought more about what Brave New Films could become, I realized that I had begun to totally move away from the traditional distribution model I had worked in for so many years. It wasn't about studios or theatres or box office grosses or TV networks any more—it was about thousands of groups, about activists, about house parties and websites and blogs and e-mail lists. Talking with Jim, learning from Wes, Joan and Eli Pariser at MoveOn, listening to Don Hazen of AlterNet (one of the wisest voices on the new media), I got it. This was the way to go, and I was excited and passionate about embracing and building on this model. There were so many stories to tell, and more and more outlets that could provide distribution for the stories, not tied to the traditional gatekeepers, decision makers, or corporate interests. Once I conceived of this broad vision of what Brave New Films could be, the possibilities became limited only by the number of hours in the day and the resources we had to produce the content of the stories.

So, why this book? Gary Baddeley, who had done such a great job distributing *Outfoxed*, suggested it before we had even fully outlined the film. Why not create a companion piece to the film, a book chronicling the project from its beginning, illuminating the process for others who might want to follow in our footsteps?

I thought long and hard about the value of opening up the process. Finally I agreed, because I realized that there were two important lessons we could and should share with others. The first is to teach others how to create and build

the high cost of low price

alternative distribution, which I firmly believe is the key to getting progressive and alternative stories told. (If you don't believe me, check with Don Hazen, the maven in this field.) The second (and perhaps harder) task is to model how to balance the political and the creative in documentary film-making. To effect change, we have to affect people, and we can only do that by telling stories both honestly and com-pellingly. Too many films miss their mark because they are too strident or heavy-handed, not trusting audiences to draw their own conclusions. I wanted the *Wal-Mart* film to be ob-sessively researched (and it is, thanks to the BNF team), and yet I also wanted it to be engaging—not to feel like home-work. Not "spinach," but a real film experience, illuminating as well as entertaining.

In fact, my good friend Danny Goldberg, a music indus-try veteran, pushed me after an early screening to engage the terrific music team that has since helped bring the strands of the film together into one cohesive whole.

With this book, Greg Spotts has illuminated enough of the process of making this film that you will be sufficiently inspired and warned regarding your own similar creative en-deavors. Of course, Greg could not spend every minute with us. He could not be at my house for the five a.m. viewing of cut sequences, or travel to every location. He was not able to write about the final editing, music, distribution, or promo-tion plans, which are still to come as I write. Yet I think that he has used his considerable skills to get behind what was go-ing on and give you an important perspective on it all, which will either inspire you or scare you off permanently from any similar undertaking.

To those who are inspired, I look forward to hearing about your plans, your efforts, your bumps along the way, and your triumphs as you pursue alternative distribution for your own films, videos, music, books, or other creative endeavors.

After you finish the book and see the film, I hope you will contact Brave New Films, at www.bravenewfilms.org, to tell us your story, share your experiences, and help us go forward together in building the kind of brave new world we all want.

– Robert Greenwald
September 2005

Wal-Mart: The High Cost of Low Price

Produced and Directed by Robert Greenwald

STAFF LIST

Producers: Jim Gilliam & Devin Smith

PRODUCTION DEPARTMENT
Coproducers: Sarah Feeley, Kerry Candaele & Caty Borum
Supervising Cinematographer: Kristy Tully
Researcher: Meleiza Figueroa
Parody Ad Producer: Laurie Levit
Parody Ad Associate Producer: Pete Carsey
Production Assistant: Zachary Freer

POSTPRODUCTION DEPARTMENT
Editors: Chris Gordon, Robert Florio, Douglas Cheek
& Jonathan Brock
Assistant Editors: Mobolaji Olambiwonnu & Lissette Roldan
Post-Production Coordinator: Jaffar Mahmood

BRAVE NEW FILMS
Principal: Rick Jacobs
Political Director: Lisa Smithline
Wal-Mart Week Coordiantor: Kabira Stokes
Outreach Coordinator: Sharaf Mowjood

WAL★MART
the high cost of low price

😈 Controlled Chaos

Robert Greenwald is too smiley to be an activist. Sitting at his large wraparound desk, he's cheery, pleasant, and positive. His wireless reading glasses are often perched atop his bald head, like an extra set of twinkling eyes that accentuate his warm and welcoming grin.

The producer of over sixty films, Robert has created a comfortable and profitable niche in the entertainment business, producing movies for network television, cable, and independent theatrical release. One of his best-known television productions is *The Burning Bed* starring Farrah Fawcett, which explored the consequences of domestic violence. At any given time, Robert has multiple movies in production for broadcast networks and cable channels.

Robert's office is filled with portraits of his heroes, from Albert Einstein to Abbie Hoffman. One of his favorite projects is *Steal This Movie*, a feature film he directed about Hoffman's life that included a re-enactment of the famous "Levitate the Pentagon" anti-war protest of October 1967.

When problems arise, Robert's reaction is mild gallows humor. He'll often spell out the worst-case scenario with light sarcasm and a grim, yet reassuring, smile. He says that the film he is now directing, a $1.6 million documentary about Wal-Mart, is "the toughest and most complex project I've ever worked on. And that includes a six-hour miniseries with Sally Field!"

The production process of the Wal-Mart film is organized in a unique way, building on Robert's experience with his two previous documentaries, *Uncovered: The Whole Truth About the Iraq War* and *Outfoxed: Rupert Murdoch's War on Journalism*. In traditional filmmaking, there are three sequential phases of a project. In preproduction, you write and research the material. In production, you shoot the footage. Finally, there's postproduction, when you edit down your many hours of footage into a ninety-minute movie.

On the Wal-Mart film, code-named the "Retail Project," all three of these phases are happening at the same time. The production effort resembles neither a scripted film nor a documentary. Rather than assembling a conventional film crew, Robert has created an aggressive news-gathering organization that is investigating the business practices of the world's largest corporation.

Wal-Mart Stores, Inc. is no stranger to controversy. The company has been accused of a wide variety of cost-saving employment practices that bend or break the law, from forcing hourly employees to work "off the clock" to using illegal immigrants as overnight cleaning crews. The largest class-action employment lawsuit in American history, *Dukes vs. Wal-Mart*, charges that the company systematically denies women the pay and promotions available to male employees.

Once primarily based in Southern, rural communities, the company has encountered fierce local resistance to an ambitious plan to expand into major cities and the West Coast.

the high cost of low price

There are entire books and websites dedicated to critiquing Wal-Mart, and the company has been the subject of protests, academic conferences, and even special elections.

There are dozens of Wal-Mart issues and controversies, and Robert Greenwald wants to explore them all. On any given week, Robert may have two or even three camera crews gathering footage in different cities. During February, March, and April, Robert's traveling crews have shot over 140 hours of original footage in ten different states. In search of stories about Wal-Mart's international operations, Robert has engaged local crews in London, Hamburg, Hong-Kong, and Quebec to conduct additional interviews.

While most of the filming is taking place out-of-town, Robert's offices in Culver City, California are jammed and buzzing. A growing staff of twenty and counting is pushing hard to finish the Retail Project by Labor Day, 2005, to accommodate an ambitious promotional campaign that is planned for November.

Two editors are working six days a week to boil down the incoming footage to manageable ten-minute segments. Although the overall structure of the film is ever-shifting, the editors are cutting and polishing individual segments that tell the story of a particular person or town.

New story ideas are investigated by two full-time researchers and a fleet of interns. If Robert wants to know where Wal-Mart has been cited for environmental violations, the research staff combs through local newspapers and TV news clips, searching for concrete examples. Robert then picks his favorite storylines, which are passed on to the co-producers for more detailed research, including telephone "pre-interviews." Once Robert and a co-producer agree that there are enough good interviewees to merit a shooting trip, a detailed shooting proposal is written for Robert to review and approve.

Robert sees the entire documentary process as a giant balancing act, trying to formulate a coherent and powerful political statement while at the same time creating an artistic and entertaining movie. He is the only member of the team who has a clear understanding of the overall project and its many moving parts. Although there are two producers and four co-producers working full-time on the film, each is focused on a particular task. None of them are charged with supervising the overall project, on either a creative or operational level.

Weekly staff meeting (from left, editor Doug Cheek, political director Lisa Smithline, and Robert Greenwald).

The organizational structure is completely flat: almost everyone reports directly to Robert, and he receives an absolute blizzard of daily e-mail from staffers seeking his direction and feedback. According to producer Jim Gilliam, who has been working with Robert since *Uncovered*, the controlled chaos is by design. "Robert needs to work this way," Jim explains. "He is unable to function effectively unless he is at the center of everything. All of us have confidence that Robert has a vision. My role as producer is to be an extension of his brain." (Robert himself does not view his process as substantially different than the way in which other directors manage big-budget films.)

WAL★MART
the high cost of low price

Robert's centrality to every aspect of the project necessitates that he stay in Culver City to manage the project on a minute-by-minute basis. Early in the process, Robert reluctantly decided that he could not go out in the field and conduct the interviews himself. The broad scope of his inquiry and the rush to complete the film by September have created a degree of separation between Robert and his topic. Rather than making his own personal journey into the heartland of America, Robert is closely supervising three co-producers who fly around the country and do the interviews.

Since Robert is not present during most of the filming, he's devised a unique way to watch the footage. With videotapes flooding in from the field by overnight mail, Robert's entire workday could be chewed up by sitting in front of a television watching the dailies in real time. So Robert directs his staff by day, and watches the new footage at night on his home computer. To save time, he often watches the footage at double-speed, with the interviewees chirping like chipmunks.

Every minute of the Retail Project's footage is available twenty-four hours a day via a password-protected website that is referred to as the "Wiki." Incoming tapes are digitized, compressed, and uploaded to the secure video server so that the researchers and co-producers can review the growing library of material within days of each new tape's arrival. While the rest of the staff watches the footage as a streaming QuickTime file, Robert gets special treatment. His home computer is programmed to automatically download new footage from the video server, so that "video dailies" are waiting for Robert on his hard drive when he gets home from the office.

The Wiki contains much more than just the raw video footage. An outside transcription service watches each new tape and uploads a word-by-word transcription to the Wiki that can be viewed by any staffer. Each one-hour videotape also has an associated set of shooting notes written by the appropriate co-producer. There's a ton of additional material on the Wiki, including Robert's original script notes, shooting settings for the Panasonic DVX-100a camera, and a huge research section with Wal-Mart-related documents, news clippings, statistics and photographs. Best of all, the Retail Project's Wiki is completely keyword searchable and is accessible from any place in the world that has internet access.

Filmmaker's Toolbox:
The Wiki

The best-known Wiki site is Wikipedia.com, "a growing online free encyclopedia being created by people all over the world who come to the site and contribute to its contents." Companies and organizations are using the same software that powers Wikipedia to create their own Wiki-enabled sites, which are often called "collaborative software" or "groupware."

A "Wiki" is a website that can be edited by everyone who uses it. Each page on a Wiki has a button called "edit page," that allows the user to add, change, or delete material. Users can also add brand-new pages and link one page to another. The idea is to create an information beehive that keeps growing and improving based on the simultaneous efforts of many individuals.

The first Wiki was created in 1995 by Ward Cunningham as a place for software programmers to share information. He called it the "WikiWikiWeb" because it sounded like "quick web." As the internet grew in popularity during the late nineties, most people

the high cost of low price

experienced the web as consumers of information published by others. Yet Cunningham's vision was to break down the barrier between publisher and reader, inviting all site users to edit, change, and add to the contents of his Wiki.

Available in a variety of inexpensive and public-domain versions, Wiki software is growing in popularity among researchers, nonprofits, and even large corporations, who find it easier to install and use than expensive "Enterprise Software" products. The Wiki's been especially useful for the Retail Project, enabling staffers at the home office and in the field to have round-the-clock access to an ever-growing library of information.

Robert's team constantly refers each other to the Wiki for information and answers. At any given time, half the computers at Robert's office complex are being used to upload or download material to the password-protected site. Since all roads lead to Robert and Robert is insanely busy, the Culver City courtyard echoes with the oft-spoken words "Hmmm, good question. Have you checked the Wiki?"

If you can't find the info you need on the Wiki, the best person to ask is co-producer Sarah Feeley, whose desk faces a large whiteboard displaying the movement of crews and equipment around the country. Sarah and the rest of the production department operate in a two-room suite that's a half-block away from Robert's main building. She and her staffers affectionately refer to their humble quarters as "the island," and the headquarters building as "the mainland." Overseeing the complexities of the Retail Project requires Sarah to walk from the island to the mainland at least once every hour.

Sarah is the type of no-nonsense woman who naturally ends up in charge of a team, and Robert describes her as "the glue that holds the whole thing together." With her wiry frame and retro-hipster wardrobe, Sarah could pass for a college student. She derives her authority not from her appearance, but from her clipped, concise pattern of speech. On a team of people who speak in paragraphs, she communicates in declarative sentences. Her motto is "just get it done."

Sarah originally came on the Retail Project for a two-week assignment before any footage had been shot, and her performance quickly made her one of Robert's most trusted lieutenants.

Her job was to figure out how to videotape fifty new Wal-Mart stores that were opening on the same day. Discovery of this Wal-Mart super-day was big news for Robert's small team of researchers, because the company provides little advance notice about its plans.

Robert had been searching for a way to illustrate the sheer scale of Wal-Mart's operations, and the opening of fifty stores on a single day seemed like the perfect opportunity. But how to shoot it?

That's where Sarah came in. Having just finished working as an associate producer on Tim Burton's new animated film *Corpse Bride*, Sarah was brought into the Retail Project on January 14 to find a way to shoot as many of the January 26 Wal-Mart store openings as possible.

Flying people around the country to twenty-seven different states would be way too expensive. So Sarah's goal was to hire a local cameraperson in each town who could shoot a grand opening with his own equipment. Many of the stores were opening in small communities, where a video professional would be hard to find.

Sarah and her two interns started phoning potential

the high cost of low price

shooters in each of the fifty places where stores were about to open. Her shooters ranged from professional freelancers in the larger markets to camcorder-toting amateurs in the smaller towns. She wanted all of her shooters to have some experience creating usable video. In some cases that experience was taping the high-school football game.

The individual shooters were offered $150 for a few hours of videotaping, and did not know they were part of a large-scale effort.

Of the fifty store openings Sarah attempted to film, she was able to get worthwhile footage on thirty-nine of them. The whole endeavor cost about $5,000, and required two weeks of Sarah's time with the help of her two full-time interns.

Robert was impressed, and immediately put Sarah to work organizing the Retail Project's first interview expeditions. After three months of work developing specific leads, researchers Caty Borum and Jenny Cartwright were champing at the bit to head out in the field and produce their own segments. Newly-titled as "co-producers," Caty and Jenny started making travel arrangements for their first trips, and Robert tasked Sarah with helping them.

After a mad rush to get Caty and Jenny out the door with the proper cameras and equipment, Sarah quickly decided that the dispatch process needed to be organized and codified. So she wrote a "field manual" describing basic procedures for planning, shooting, and wrapping each field expedition, procedures that have become the basic rules-of-the-road of the Retail Project.

The cover of Sarah's field manual bears a quote from one of her film school professors: "There are a million reasons why something can't be done. We are here to find the one reason why it can."

Sarah is the only person other than Robert with a complete picture of the week-to-week status of Robert's investigative effort. Using the Wiki, she's keeping track of each of Robert's "story buckets," from "Shopkeeper" to "Employee Health Care." Some stories are being pursued by just one co-producer. Others are based on the hundreds of hours of archival news footage that's been collected. The more complicated stories are being pursued by the entire investigative team under Robert's close supervision.

Sarah says she's running as tight a ship as possible without overly disturbing Robert's controlled chaos. "The way this project started out, we've been racing to catch up the entire time," she explains. "We got out of the gate before sufficient planning had been done. The co-producers are under a lot of pressure from Robert to find great stories and get those stories on tape. My area is all the crap people don't want to get pushed about—dotting the i's and crossing the t's."

Sarah is in charge of logistics, equipment, and expenses for the co-producers. Prior to moving forward with each shoot, the co-producers must submit to Sarah a production plan and budget. Once Sarah signs off on a shoot budget, it goes to producer Devin Smith for final approval.

Although she is the main person reviewing individual shooting budgets, Sarah finds it curious that she knows so little about the budget of the entire film. "This movie operates unlike any film I've ever worked on before," Sarah explains. "I have never seen a master budget for this project. I don't even know if such a thing exists. We're still raising some of the production money, and I don't know if we're spending money that's in the bank, spending money we don't have or spending Robert's personal money."

the high cost of low price

😈 Confronting the President

Robert's admiration of the rebellious Abbie Hoffman is the one indication that a smiley, five-foot-six Hollywood producer would end up challenging the national security establishment of the United States. On the heels of America's March 20, 2003 invasion of Iraq, Robert rush-produced his first documentary film, *Uncovered: The Whole Truth About the Iraq War*. The sixty-minute film was sharply critical of President Bush and senior members of his administration.

The genesis of Robert's opposition to the Iraq War was a presentation by former UN Weapons Inspector Scott Ritter that Robert attended in the fall of 2002. What started as an e-mail message from Robert to some of his friends in film and television quickly grew into Artists United to Win Without War, a group Robert co-founded with actor Mike Farrell.

On December 15, 2002, Artists United ran a full-page anti-war advertisement in the *New York Times*, signed by over one hundred actors and musicians including Martin Sheen, Matt Damon, Ethan Hawke, Samuel L. Jackson, and Dave

Matthews. Written as an open letter, the ad concluded with a statement that was virtually the opposite of the Bush administration position: "The valid US and UN objective of disarming Saddam Hussein can be achieved through legal diplomatic means. There is no need for war. Let us instead devote our resources to improving the security and well-being of people here at home and around the world."

Although Robert had been active in various Los Angeles area nonprofits, he had never before gotten involved in a leadership role on national political issues. As he and Farrell coordinated the activities of Artists United with the efforts of other anti-war groups, Robert started to meet a variety of politicians, organizers, and activists far outside the world of entertainment.

One of the organizations supporting the *Times* ad was MoveOn.org, an online activist group that had been pressing the Bush administration to "Let the Inspections Work" since July 2002. Robert got to know MoveOn founder Wes Boyd during a series of conference calls to coordinate the "Win Without War" coalition, which encompassed a broad range of organizations including the Sierra Club, the NAACP, Greenpeace, Rainbow/Push, and several faith-based groups. The relationship forged between Robert and Wes during this pre-war period would become a crucial part of Robert's subsequent efforts.

The idea for *Uncovered* was born three months into the US-led invasion of Iraq, when Robert noticed a subtle yet significant change in the Bush administration's statements about Saddam Hussein. Instead of talking about Hussein's weapons of mass destruction, government officials had begun to use the words "weapons programs." To Robert, this shift in verbiage was a signal that, although President Bush had already declared "mission accomplished," no actual weapons of mass destruction were likely to be found in Iraq by the American search teams.

the high cost of low price

At the same time, Robert began reading about former CIA analyst Ray McGovern, who told the *New York Times* that the intelligence community was "totally demoralized." McGovern was a member of Veteran Intelligence Professionals for Sanity, a group that called the invasion of Iraq a "policy and intelligence fiasco of monumental proportions." Robert thought McGovern's group could be a source for credible experts for a documentary film about the run-up to the Iraq war.

Without a formal budget or distribution plan, Robert began directing his first documentary in July 2003. The small initial team included co-producers Kate McArdle and Jim Gilliam and editor Chris Gordon. (Kate worked with Robert on Artists United, *Uncovered,* and *Outfoxed.* The Retail Project marks the third consecutive Robert Greenwald project for Jim and Chris.)

Constructed with the sequential logic of a geometry proof, Robert's script outline paired public statements by George Bush, Dick Cheney, Donald Rumsfeld, and Condoleezza Rice with point-by-point rebuttals from McGovern, Ritter, and a growing panel of retired intelligence and foreign policy professionals. A local crew videotaped most of the experts in hotel rooms in Washington, DC, with Robert asking the questions either in person or from Culver City via speakerphone.

Filmmaker's Toolbox:
Film vs. Digital

With over thirty years experience shooting movies on traditional 35mm film, Robert loves the look and feel of high-end moviemaking. Yet for *Uncovered*, he decided to use the inexpensive digital video cameras that have been revolutionizing documentary production since the late nineties.

Pioneered by Sony and Panasonic in 1995, the MiniDV format was designed for consumer handycams and was not intended as a professional tool. Yet, in 1997, Canon released the XL-1, a heavyweight "pro-sumer" MiniDV camera with interchangeable lenses, and before long people started to make movies with it. Eliminating the high cost of film and processing, digital video enabled documentary filmmakers to shoot and store large amounts of footage on hour-long tapes that cost less than ten dollars apiece.

At first, television networks sniffed at MiniDV productions, claiming that the consumer format was not "broadcast quality." Yet fans of documentaries did not seem to mind, and over time MiniDV videos began airing on cable and appearing on DVD. The sea change in production methods reached critical mass in 2002, when the documentary *Spellbound*, shot by first-time filmmakers on a Canon XL-1, generated five million dollars at the box office and was nominated for an Oscar.

One year later, Panasonic released its own "pro-sumer" MiniDV camera, the DVX-100, with special features designed to make digital video look more like traditional film. Priced at less than $4,000, the camera has become a hit with documentary filmmakers, and its newest version, the DVX-100a, is currently Robert's camera-of-choice for documentary projects.

the high cost of low price

What started as an informal, small-scale effort became increasingly complex and expensive, and soon Robert realized he would need outside funding in order to complete the project. Reaching out to his new friend Wes Boyd, Robert asked if MoveOn.org would be willing to contribute fifty thousand dollars towards the production costs and become an official "presenter" of the movie. Wes agreed, and urged Robert to finish the film as quickly as possible.

Shortly thereafter, Robert contacted former Clinton administration chief-of-staff John Podesta, who was in the process of starting up a new think tank called the Center for American Progress. Robert offered Podesta the opportunity to become another official presenter of the film, and Podesta accepted. Beyond providing completion funding for the movie, the Center for American Progress became an important conduit to the "inside the beltway" public policy establishment.

At the onset of these new relationships, Robert did not have a specific plan for precisely how MoveOn and the Center for American Progress would help his film find an audience. Yet Robert already knew that the traditional entertainment distribution pattern would not be effective for *Uncovered*. First and foremost, Robert's goal was to get his message out as quickly as possible, hoping to influence public perception of a fast-moving issue. The typical route of submitting the documentary to film festivals and waiting for an answer would be far too slow for this project. Even if a high-profile festival premiere could be obtained, it offered no guarantee that a film distribution company would take notice and agree to release Robert's documentary in theaters.

In fact, the controversial nature of his subject matter made Robert skeptical that film distributors and theater owners would be willing to touch it. Accusing the President of the United States of being dishonest with the American people is not exactly a way to win friends and influence people in the increasingly corporate world of movie distribution. Having seen the power of MoveOn to generate a million signatures for an anti-war petition back in March, Robert had a feeling that MoveOn could create a rapid and unusual campaign to connect his film to a politically-activated audience. At the same time, the Center for American Progress could build a buzz among politicians, foreign policy specialists, and other Washington insiders.

Uncovered made its debut on November 3, 2003, at a time when the mainstream media was still solidly in support of Operation Iraqi Freedom. The first public screenings of *Uncovered* were organized by the Center for American Progress, taking place in Washington on November 3, New York on November 4, and Los Angeles on November 11.

Receiving little press coverage, *Uncovered* could have been a political non-event. Yet the innovative campaign Robert and Wes designed for MoveOn.org was wildly successful. On the same day as the Washington, DC world premiere screening, the MoveOn website began offering the *Uncovered* DVD as a premium to members who pledged thirty dollars or more. Response to MoveOn's November 3 e-mail blast was immediate and overwhelming, generating 8,000 individual pledges within the first three hours. Three days later, the total number of pledges exceeded 20,000, and by the end of November, MoveOn had distributed nearly 30,000 *Uncovered* DVDs, raising almost one million dollars to be used in MoveOn's future campaigns against the Iraq war.

The Nation magazine and two internet news portals, Alternet and Buzzflash, also offered the DVD for sale on their websites during the same time period, broadening the reach of the initial campaign. In addition, Alternet brought the film to their home base of San Francisco, sponsoring a screening on November 19.

As fall turned to winter, the *Uncovered* DVD became a tal-

the high cost of low price

isman of sorts for Americans who felt lied to by their president. The structured critique offered by Robert's experts was a concise and memorable alternative to the Bush war narrative. As DVDs were passed from person to person, so was Robert's message. Sharing the film with a friend or co-worker became a small act of protest against the war.

It soon became clear that MoveOn members and readers of *The Nation*, Alternet and Buzzflash were just the tip of the iceberg of the potential audience for a serious and thoughtful anti-war film. As public awareness grew, an opportunity arose to add a conventional distribution channel into the mix. The Disinformation Company, an independent publisher best known for edgy nonfiction books, made a deal with Robert to commercially release the *Uncovered* DVD in retail stores and on Amazon.com.

Meanwhile, the MoveOn team decided to create a second phase of their *Uncovered* campaign. Staffer Eli Pariser came up with the idea of encouraging MoveOn members to host *Uncovered* "house parties" to show the movie to their friends and co-workers. Hoping to generate a few hundred screenings, MoveOn sent out an e-mail solicitation inviting members to sign up to host screenings on the first Sunday in December. Exceeding all expectations, over 2,600 members hosted screenings in their homes and at community venues, creating a nationwide exhibition of Robert's movie on a single night, December 7. Without being advertised in newspapers or exhibited in conventional movie theaters, *Uncovered* had found a new way to be seen in cities and towns across the country.

Two months later, the political environment changed rapidly when US weapons inspector David Kay resigned. Summarizing his nine months of experience searching postwar Iraq for signs of biological, chemical, and nuclear weapons, Kay told National Public Radio that "based on what I've seen, we're very unlikely to find large stockpiles of weapons. I don't think they exist." The mainstream media gradually re-discovered their collective backbone and began to revisit the issues Greenwald's film had raised in October 2003. (Green-wald later interviewed David Kay on camera for an expanded 2004 version of *Uncovered.*)

On May 24, 2004, the *New York Times* published an extraordinary editorial lamenting the paper's timid and unquestioning coverage of the Bush administration's pre-war claims. "Looking back, we wish we had been more aggressive in re-examining the claims as new evidence emerged—or failed to emerge," lamented the editorial board. Out on a limb in the fall of 2003, Robert and his experts were now vindicated by the "Newspaper of Record." Beyond the impact of his political message, Robert's innovative "alternative distribution" methods had created a powerful new template to connect timely documentaries with a passionate audience.

the high cost of low price

😈 Refining the Model

By the time the *New York Times* issued its historic "mea culpa," Robert already had a new target in his documentary sights. Personally raising hell had proved to be far more satisfying than making biopics about people who'd raised hell in the past. Working with many of the same folks who helped him make *Uncovered*, Robert spent the spring of 2004 putting the finishing touches on his movie about the right-wing bias of the Fox News Channel.

Robert's new documentary was being made in complete secrecy, so that the powerful News Corporation would be taken by complete surprise when the film was released. With the incendiary title *Outfoxed: Rupert Murdoch's War on Journalism,* Robert's work-in-progress was bound to raise the ambient temperature in the News Corp executive suite.

In the same way that *Uncovered* rebutted the Bush administration's pre-war claims, *Outfoxed* was designed as a frontal attack on the "Fair and Balanced" slogan that is plastered on Fox News programming. To gather ammunition for his case,

Robert assembled a group of volunteer "newshounds" who watched and taped Fox News around the clock, searching for patterns of bias. Recruited by MoveOn and working from private homes across the country, the newshounds identified coverage patterns and particular clips that became the backbone of *Outfoxed*. (This complex and unusual production process is documented in the "Behind the Scenes" bonus feature on the *Outfoxed* DVD.)

Editing down this mountain of Fox News footage was a colossal task that required far more man-hours and money than Robert had originally expected. Rather than being edited by one person, the film required five full-time editors, three working day shifts and two working nights. As production costs soared above $200,000, Robert took out a personal loan to fund the completion of the film.

Yet the risk of losing money was only one of Robert's concerns. The big risk was a massive lawsuit by News Corporation, who had recently sued Al Franken for trademark infringement. Franken's book *Lies and the Lying Liars Who Tell Them: A Fair and Balanced Look at the Right* was targeted by News Corp's lawyers not for defamation or slander, but for appropriating the intellectual property of Fox's trademarked phrase "Fair and Balanced." News Corp attempted to suppress publication of Franken's book, but was rebuffed by a federal judge who called the company's legal action "wholly without merit, both factually and legally."

If Fox News Channel was bent out of shape about the satirical use of its slogan in a book title, imagine how it might react to a sharply critical documentary that used dozens and dozens of clips from Fox's copyrighted telecasts. Robert hoped to avoid a lawsuit on the grounds that his inclusion of the Fox News clips was protected by the doctrine of "fair use." According to US copyright law, "the fair use of a copyrighted work for purposes such as criticism, comment, news report-

the high cost of low price

ing, teaching, scholarship, or research, is not an infringement of copyright."

Attorney Lawrence Lessig volunteered to advise Robert on the legal issues raised by his film. The author of several books that explore the changing nature of copyright in a digital age, Lessig believes that fair use is an essential enabler of an open and free democracy. On July 11, 2004, Lessig posted an item on his blog about the political and legal issues raised by *Out-foxed*. "As with news-gathering, critical political filmmaking needs a buffer zone of protection against the overreaching of the law. And if the potential of this medium—now liberated by digital technology—is to be realized, we need clear precedents that establish that critics have the freedom to criticize without having to hire a lawyer first." (Until such time as the courts have decided a greater number of fair use cases involving documentary films, filmmakers should continue to seek legal advice about the particular content in each of their films.)

One of the factors News Corp would be considering in a decision whether or not to sue would be a desire to avoid the miserable publicity that the company suffered on the heels of their unsuccessful Franken suit. Standard procedure in corporate damage control is to avoid calling attention to your critics, and the Franken suit did exactly the opposite, serving as a high-profile launch to Franken's book, which became a bestseller.

Again paired with MoveOn.org and the Center for American Progress, Robert planned to release *Outfoxed* on DVD on July 13, 2004, with hundreds of Sunday-night house party screenings occurring five days later. The goal was to keep *Out-foxed* under wraps until the absolute last moment, giving Fox News a minimal amount of time to plan a counterattack. Yet behind the scenes, Robert had lined up a powerful roster of partners for a multi-pronged, simultaneous unveiling. From media reform organizations to DVD publisher Disinformation, everybody was working together to create a high-profile "opening" for the movie, drawing on the various alternative techniques developed the previous year to promote *Uncovered*. Re-imagining a concept drawn from the marketing of big-budget entertainment films, Robert and his team envisioned a splashy launch based on hard-news controversy rather than red-carpet glamour.

Robert and his partners successfully kept their battle plan under wraps, and the existence of *Outfoxed* was generally unknown until the June 11 publication of a Sunday *New York Times Magazine* story about Greenwald's political filmmaking. Entitled "How to Make a Guerilla Documentary," the article called Robert's upcoming Fox News documentary "an obsessively researched expose," and recapped Robert's earlier achievements with *Uncovered*. Officials from Fox News declined to comment about *Outfoxed* for the *Times Magazine* story.

Filmmaker's Toolbox:
Working With Nonprofits and Political Groups

Independent filmmakers often approach Robert for advice on how to get their film to the public via nonprofit groups and other political and social organizations. His answer begins with a warning. "You cannot expect an organization to distribute your film, because it's simply not their job. Their job is to affect social and political change."

Robert believes that involving organizations early in a film project is crucial. "You want to bring in your partners while you are still making the film, which gives you time to get in synch on everything from the political message of the film itself to the timing and techniques

that will be used in the grass-roots campaign."

Emphasizing that alternative distribution really is an *alternative* to the traditional entertainment channels, Robert tells filmmakers with grass-roots aspirations to expect to forego the ego-gratification of the indie film circuit. "You can't have everything. If you want a splashy premiere at a major festival and an art house theater run, then you should go for it. If you want to create social change, then you make a different set of choices and focus on working with groups that can help make change happen."

One of the big questions facing political filmmakers is whether they are looking for a sequential or a simultaneous rollout of their film. Traditional entertainment distribution is based on the idea that each distribution channel is made available during an exclusive window. First the film can be seen in theaters. Then it becomes available on DVD and pay-per-view. Later, the film is shown on advertiser-supported television. As time passes, it becomes cheaper and easier for a viewer to experience the film, enticing additional customers who may not have been willing to make a special trip to the movie theater.

Yet films dealing with timely social and political issues can lose a significant amount of their impact over time. One of Robert's primary innovations has been to simultaneously release his political films in as many channels and formats as possible, creating a white-hot moment of publicity and political activation.

Yet Fox News spokeswoman Irena Briganti had plenty to say to *Washington Post* media columnist Howard Kurtz, who published two separate stories about *Outfoxed* on the same day as the *Times Magazine* piece. The larger story, published on page D1 of the *Post*, was a critical review of the film itself, yet the essence of the Fox News counterattack was contained in the smaller story on page D6. Entitled "Too Late to Comment?" the story raised the possibility that *Times Magazine* writer Robert Boynton had colluded with Greenwald to ambush Fox News. Apparently Fox didn't like that they were first contacted by Boynton on June 29, giving them seventy-two hours to reply with a comment before Boynton's July 1 deadline.

The notion of when exactly the *Times* first contacted Fox News about *Outfoxed* was a tempest in a teapot, but controversy breeds press coverage. On Monday, June 12, Robert and his partner organizations held an *Outfoxed* press conference at the Ritz Carlton Hotel in New York City, with dozens of major media outlets in attendance. Fox News handed out an angrily-worded statement about *Outfoxed* to journalists as they left the hotel. Upset about everything from late notification to footage theft to "liberal" fund-raising sources, Fox News made sure that journalists had a full range of exciting controversies to write about, proving that television people are far better at pumping up a story than tamping it down.

Outfoxed made its official premiere the very next evening, at the New School for Social Research in New York City. The premiere included a panel discussion on media bias featuring columnist Arianna Huffington, John Podesta of the Center for American Progress, and Eric Alterman, media columnist for *The Nation*. The *Outfoxed* DVD was commercially released by Disinformation on the same day. Riding a three-day wave of national publicity, *Outfoxed* instantly became the top selling DVD at Amazon.com.

At the end of the week, the grass-roots campaign kicked

the high cost of low price

into action, as over 3,000 MoveOn members hosted *Outfoxed* house parties on Sunday, July 18. The plan was similar to the *Uncovered* house parties of November 2003, but this time journalists were paying attention. Writers from dozens of daily and weekly newspapers attended the house parties and published stories about the grass-roots enthusiasm for the film. On July 19, the *San Francisco Chronicle* reported that 382 house parties took place in the Bay Area alone.

Learning the lesson from the Franken fiasco, the mighty News Corporation kept its lawyers in check and took no legal action against *Outfoxed*, fearful of creating even more publicity about the movie. Yet the legendary anger of Fox News commentator Bill O'Reilly could not be contained.

On August 5, the night before *Outfoxed* made its theatrical debut in four cities, O'Reilly referred to Robert as a "smear merchant" on "The O'Reilly Factor," his prime-time TV show. Five days later, the Quad Cinema in Manhattan reported that *Outfoxed* achieved the highest-grossing opening weekend in the theater's thirty-year history, which motivated independent theaters in additional cities to exhibit the film.

The theatrical release of *Outfoxed* was unplanned, an outgrowth of a completely separate effort to bring *Uncovered* to a wider audience. Earlier in 2004, Robert had made a deal with Cinema Libre Studio to bring an expanded version of *Uncovered* to indie movie theaters in late summer. As Cinema Libre was ramping up for *Uncovered*'s August 20 theatrical debut, the *Outfoxed* controversy broke wide open. Cinema Libre's publicity-savvy Phillipe Diaz decided to rush-release *Outfoxed* in theaters, even though it was already available on DVD. So instead of having one Greenwald film in theaters in the summer of 2004, Cinema Libre had two.

The synchronicity was perfect. The mainstream press, who had missed the boat on *Uncovered* the first time around, rediscovered the film in the context of Robert's highly-publicized success with *Outfoxed*. In the summer of 2004, both *Outfoxed* and *Uncovered* were widely reviewed, and *Outfoxed* sold over 200,000 DVDs in the process, proving the commercial potential of Robert's unconventional filmmaking.

Like his hero Abbie Hoffman, Robert had tapped into the spirit of a new era and created his own form of "political theater." He appeared on dozens of television and radio programs and was lauded for both the message of his films and the innovative hybrid of alt-media and big-media he had used to find his audience. Sales of the two DVDs enabled Robert to pay back his loans. And the converted Culver City motel that was once a quiet production office for television "movies-of-the-week" had become the teeming hive of a new generation of media-activists, ready to attack whatever subject Robert dreamed up for his next political documentary.

the high cost of low price

😊 Cash or Charge?

Wal-Mart will be hiring over 100,000 new employees in the US this year, and Jenny Cartwright wants to be one of them. She's interviewing for an entry-level cashier position at a Wal-Mart Supercenter.

Jenny's first interview at the Supercenter is going well. The assistant manager likes the fact that Jenny is available to work nights and weekends. Jenny has previous experience in retail, and seems like someone who puts the customer's needs first. Her references have checked out, and her high score on a detailed pre-employment questionnaire indicates that she's likely to fit in with Wal-Mart's unique corporate culture. Near the end of the interview, the assistant manager leans over and gushes with a smile, "It's almost too good to be true!"

Jenny smiles back. The manager tells Jenny she's hired, and that her retail experience will enable her to start at an hourly rate considerably higher than the usual starting wage. The manager makes Jenny's seven dollars an hour salary sound like an achievement.

Within a few days, Jenny is ringing up customers. Her first week is supposed to be for training and computer-based learning, but the store is shorthanded and the managers quickly put her to work. Her fellow cashiers tell her to enjoy her "honeymoon period," when the managers are nice and the breaks come right on time.

Jenny takes her new job seriously. She's convinced herself to be "the best cashier this store has ever seen," and is committed to solving customers' problems and giving service with a smile. Two assistant managers notice her positive attitude, and start "cross training" her in their departments. One of them later tells her "it's so rare to find a warm body with a brain around here."

The next day, the two assistant managers are arguing over Jenny in full view of the customers. Both assistant managers want her to work for them, even though she has been hired to do cashier work at a cashier's pay scale. Between the cash register, the two departments, and all the training, Jenny realizes she hasn't been getting her breaks. The store seems chronically understaffed.

Friday rolls around, and Jenny participates in her first "Friday meeting." Half idea session, half pep rally, the Friday meeting is fueled by lots of enthusiasm and cheering. Jenny hopes her new co-workers don't notice her mild attempts at applause. Unbeknownst to her fellow Wal-Mart associates, Jenny is a co-producer of the Retail Project and is living at a nearby motel. Her assignment for the month is to get to know her co-workers in the hopes that one of them will agree to star in Robert Greenwald's new documentary. (The name Jenny Cartwright is a pseudonym.)

Jenny was the first person that Robert hired for the Retail Project, back in November of 2004. She had recently produced a "clip show" that featured lots of archival footage, and Robert expected to use plenty of news clips and archival

video in the Wal-Mart film.

Jenny signed on a few days before the Wal-Mart movie's first production meeting. One week earlier, new documentaries about Wal-Mart had aired on CNBC and PBS. According to producer Jim Gilliam, who had spent the previous two weeks doing some preliminary Wal-Mart research, both of the existing Wal-Mart teledocs left him wanting more. "The CNBC show was essentially a puff-piece, giving Wal-Mart's CEO Lee Scott a platform to respond to his critics," he says. "*Frontline*, on the other hand, was too intellectual, preaching only to the converted."

The first production meeting, which took place in Robert's office on November 18, 2004, included Jenny, Jim, producer Devin Smith, researcher Meleiza Figueroa, and Robert's political director, Lisa Smithline. Devin, Jim, and Lisa had worked with Robert on *Outfoxed*, and he envisioned them as the core employees of Brave New Films, his newly-formed production company. From now on, Robert Greenwald Productions would exclusively work on scripted projects, and Brave New Films would produce Robert's documentaries, video shorts, and other forms of media addressing political and social issues. Robert hoped that Brave New Films could develop the talents of his key staffers over the long term, building collective expertise in both digital production and grass-roots activism.

Robert told the assembled group that the first Brave New Films project would be a documentary about Wal-Mart. His vision for the film was very different than *Uncovered* and *Outfoxed*. Instead of using experts as "talking heads," Robert wanted to focus on the personal stories of Wal-Mart's employees and the local shopkeepers who compete with Wal-Mart. Ideally, one or more of Wal-Mart's "associates" could be filmed over a period of time, revealing the challenges they faced supporting their families on less than ten dollars an hour.

Robert wanted the Wal-Mart movie to be appealing to small-town America, particularly the "red" states, and he felt that personal stories would be the best way to accomplish that goal. The movie Robert held up as a beacon of inspiration was the award-winning documentary *Hoop Dreams*. Shot over a period of four years, *Hoop Dreams* follows teenage basketball players William Gates and Arthur Agee as they pursue a shot at NBA glory. The film takes the viewer on a roller coaster ride of high hopes and economic hardship, revealing larger truths about the forgotten corners of the ghetto through the struggles of two African-American families.

Filmmaker's Toolbox: Internet Research

By the time Robert "locks picture" on the Retail Project, his lead researcher, Meleiza Figueroa, will have spent nine months investigating Wal-Mart as a full-time job. Using Google and Lexis-Nexis as her primary tools, Meleiza continuously refines her work process and her techniques, with the goal of finding the richest, most detailed information as quickly as possible. In her quest to provide answers to Robert and the co-producers, Meleiza also peruses academic studies and sometimes contacts the authors directly for additional information. She explains:

There are two basic principles I live by when searching, on Google as well as elsewhere:

1. Read every word! A lot of articles contain little tidbits that may prove useful later. The more

articles I read rather than skim, the more I start to pick up patterns of recurring names, phrases, and sources. I then use these recurring words to further refine my searches. For example, "Wal-Mart healthcare" becomes "Wal-Mart healthcare CHIP SCHIP dependents" or "Wal-Mart healthcare public assistance Representative George Miller."

2. Save everything to disc! Many times, bits of info I picked up in the early stages of research became critically important later in the project, when more specific stuff was needed. I also bookmark every useful site that I encounter, building a library of sources that can be accessed as necessary.

I also enjoyed the benefit of a subscription to Lexis-Nexis, a pricey research tool that can search newspapers and TV news broadcasts dating back ten years or more. (Factiva offers a less expensive news archive for individual users.)

The great thing about Lexis-Nexis is the versatility it has with customizing searches. My best friends in a Lexis-Nexis search have been the wildcard, and the search terms "and" and "or." When looking for video clips on crimes in Wal-Mart parking lots, I used variations of the following phrase: "Wal-Mart and parking lot and rob! or rape! or assault! or shoot! or stab! or carjack! or kidnap! or abduct!"

Morbid as that search was (and it saddened me to see how many crimes have taken place), this particular search phrase allowed me to find material about a variety of different crimes that occurred in Wal-Mart parking lots. If I needed sound bites, I could add the word "interview" to my search phrase.

Robert told Jenny and Meleiza to make it their mission to find Wal-Mart families whose experiences could be filmed over a multi-month period with a "fly-on-the-wall" camera. "People are shocked that Wal-Mart employees are paid so little that they not only qualify for government aid, Wal-Mart helps them get it," he told the assembled group. Robert found it incredible that in 2004, America's largest corporation was sponging off the government safety net instead of creating good jobs that improved people's lives. "When I first heard this, I knew I had to dramatize it by finding a living, breathing employee, so that the audience could really grasp the reality of a billion dollar corporation steering its own employees to government aid."

Jenny left the meeting feeling energized for the investigation ahead. There were over a million Wal-Mart employees in the US, and the most logical place to start would be the *Dukes* case. Surely one of the plaintiffs accusing Wal-Mart of gender discrimination would be willing to welcome a camera crew into her life for a few months.

Jenny began calling women who were working at Wal-Mart and simultaneously suing the company as *Dukes* case plaintiffs. She combed through the leads for Robert's ideal candidate: a single mother working at Wal-Mart and collecting public assistance.

the high cost of low price

Although the various women Jenny called were pleasant and helpful, they were universally unwilling to appear on camera. Their fears were palpable: fear of losing their jobs, fear of revealing their personal lives to the camera, and, most powerfully, a fear of what their small-town neighbors might think of someone who badmouthed their employer in a film.

As December turned to January, Jenny, Meleiza, and newly hired researcher Caty Borum tried everything to find that "current employee" who could anchor a major portion of the Wal-Mart film. Identifying Wal-Mart associates who fit the profile was easy, yet each promising lead quickly hit the same roadblock: fear.

Meanwhile, other stories came to the surface that were ready to be filmed. Jenny and Caty were promoted to co-producers in February, and started flying around the country gathering material.

By mid-March, the Retail Project had moved from the research phase into full production mode. Yet Robert's "A-story," the current employee on public assistance, still had not been located. If the film was going to follow a current employee for a period of time, that filming would need to start soon. Time was running out on the *Hoop Dreams* concept.

So Jenny decided to go undercover. How better to get to know current employees of Wal-Mart than to become a Wal-Mart associate herself?

WAL★MART
the high cost of low price

☺ Early Outings

Co-producer Caty Borum has been researching Wal-Mart longer than anyone else on Robert's crew. In the summer of 2004, Caty was running an online voter registration project and researching Wal-Mart during her spare time. Her goal was to direct a documentary about Wal-Mart, and she needed to write a treatment before seeking production funds.

A few weeks prior to the election, Caty and Robert heard about each other's Wal-Mart projects and decided to meet for lunch. Both had done some initial research, but neither had shot any footage. Although Caty would have loved to direct a Wal-Mart documentary herself, she offered her research to Robert and told him she was available to help out in any way she could. The most important thing was getting the movie made, and Caty saw that Robert was much better positioned to assemble a crew and move forward quickly.

So it felt like karmic payback that within three months Caty became Robert's eyes and ears in the field. Traveling with supervising cinematographer Kristy Tully, Caty has pursued stories in Ohio, North Carolina, Virginia, Arkansas, and Missouri. While Jenny has concentrated much of her time "embedding" as a Wal-Mart associate, Caty and Kristy have been Robert's rapid response team, exploring small-town America in a series of short trips.

Back in February, the first month of shooting, Robert and his team tried a variety of approaches to the fieldwork. Robert wanted a consistent look to the footage, so his goal was to have Kristy shoot as much of it as possible. In the beginning, Robert thought that the researchers could develop the stories by phone and then Kristy could go out alone for the shoot, limiting the travel costs of each field trip. But conducting an interview while operating camera and sound proved to be too much responsibility for one person.

The first shooting expeditions also demonstrated that interviewees responded best when the same person who talked to them on the phone arrived in their hometown. The rapport developed by the co-producers on the telephone was wasted if someone different showed up to shoot the actual interview. Sending two people into the field for each shoot doubled the cost of acquiring footage, putting major pressure on Robert's original budget.

Although technical and logistical bugs were still being worked out, important footage was collected in the early days of the project. Jenny's "anti-union" story played out with great drama in late February. Competition was fierce as the national media swarmed Loveland, Colorado to cover a grass-roots effort to unionize the auto repair department of a single Wal-Mart store. Yet Jenny and Kristy had arranged for special access to worker/organizer Josh Noble, capturing great behind-the-scenes material including Josh's late-night phone calls to shore up support among his co-workers, the seizure he suffered just hours before the vote, and public

the high cost of low price

reaction to the devastating seventeen-to-one vote against forming a union.

Caty scored her own February coup with the story of H&H Hardware, a family-run business in Middlefield, Ohio. Caty discovered H&H at the perfect time, because the Wal-Mart in Middlefield was still under construction. The unfolding story seemed like a great opportunity to capture action as it occurred, rather than interview people about things that had happened in the past.

Caty made her first trip to Middlefield on February 10, 2005. It was one of the Retail Project's earliest field expeditions, and still ranks as one of the best. Kristy the cinematographer was on the road with Jenny, so Caty went to Middlefield with a substitute cameraman. The setting was unusual and evocative: Middlefield Village is in Amish Country, and it's not uncommon to see horse drawn buggies parked alongside Chevys and Fords in the main shopping district.

H&H Hardware turned out to be a rather large store anchoring its own little shopping center. Owned and operated by John Hunter, the business was started way back in 1962 by Don Hunter, John's father. Members of the National Rifle Association, the Hunters were indeed

Second-generation hardware store owner John Hunter.

avid hunters, and registered Republicans as well. Their store had a thriving sporting goods section selling rifles and other hunting-related gear.

Wal-Mart's impending arrival was already causing problems for the Hunters. Attempting to refinance their commercial mortgage, the Hunters were met with stiff resistance from the local banks. Rather than appreciating, the

Hunters' building and the land beneath it were losing value. According to local appraisers, the real-estate market was anticipating a decline in downtown business activity as soon as Wal-Mart opened.

The Hunter family welcomed Caty and her cameraman into their world with great warmth and hospitality. Caty was invited to film the Hunters at work and at play, and she quickly became fond of the Hunters' quirky group of long-time employees.

Filmmaker's Toolbox: Creative Choices for Shooting

Rather than using local crews of varying skills and styles, Robert decided to hire Kristy Tully as supervising cinematographer for the Retail Project, in the hope that she could shoot as much of the movie as possible. Kristy worked closely with Robert on developing an initial creative plan for the visuals, a plan that considered both the footage itself and the impact of the filmmaking process on the people in front of the camera.

Robert and I wanted the personal stories to feel like a film, rather than a TV program or a commercial. Our goal was for the film to seem raw, like stripped-down reality. Robert believes that the only way to counter Wal-Mart's multimillion dollar ad campaigns is to feature real people in their real lives: no makeup, diffusion filters, or camera tricks.

One of the great technical advances with the small MiniDV cameras is their ability to shoot in

low light conditions. We wanted everything to feel as natural as possible, and avoided using professional lights whenever possible. When we did add light, the goal would be to enhance what was happening naturally, rather than change it. To create an intimate feeling with the subjects, we tried to bring as little equipment and crew into their homes as possible.

When we arrived at a location, I would start with a quick survey of the house, office, barn, or backyard, looking at how the natural light was falling. We'd try to include personal details in the frame; kitchens, desks, and living rooms revealed subtle details of people's lives, adding layers of texture to the film. Personal stories were generally filmed with a handheld camera, and B-roll of cities, towns, and farms was shot with the camera on a tripod.

We did encounter a few topics we felt should be shot very simply, with a person sitting in a chair and the camera on a tripod. Two examples are crime victim Laura Tanaka, and former Wal-Mart executive Jim Lynn, both of whom tell emotional stories to the camera with a minimum of visual distraction.

Filming the H&H staffers talking to the camera while going about their work seemed like a great way to experiment with the naturalistic shooting style Robert and Kristy had requested. Yet when Kristy reviewed the footage a week later, she was deeply disappointed with its look and feel.

The simultaneous pursuit of multiple stories meant Kristy couldn't be in two places at once, but training other camera operators to work within Kristy's creative guidelines was going to be difficult.

Visuals aside, the H&H Hardware footage was exactly the kind of story Robert wanted in his film. On her way out of town, Caty asked the Hunters if she could return in a month to see how H&H was faring. The timing was looking perfect for Caty to witness Wal-Mart's opening and its consequences on the Hunter family business.

By the time Caty returned to Ohio four weeks later, H&H Hardware was already closing its doors. With sources of capital drying up and the property losing value, the Hunters had decided to make an orderly shutdown of their business. Rather than push all their chips to the middle of the table for an epic battle with Wal-Mart, the Hunters decided that they just didn't hold the cards to compete. The Middlefield Wal-Mart store opened two months later and became a national story, since it was the first Wal-Mart ever to have special parking spots for Amish horse-drawn buggies.

During the second trip, Caty got a ton of footage of the Hunters and their employees feeling sad amid their final clearance sale, plus excellent B-roll of construction at the Wal-Mart site. Caty found herself feeling profoundly moved by the Hunters and their loss. "During the clearance sale, I saw aunts and uncles working the registers and stocking shelves: Everyone was pitching in to help. You really got the feeling of how deeply the store was woven into the fabric of the entire extended family."

Caty's experience with the Hunters was an early sign that the *Hoop Dreams* "fly on the wall" method is extremely difficult to pull off. It requires a huge investment of time and money, burning up tape while waiting for something to happen. Even when the camera crew is in

the right place at the right time, it's quite possible that a promising situation fizzles out, rather than building to a compelling climax.

Meanwhile, co-producer Jenny Cartwright is still searching for the climax of her undercover mission as a Wal-Mart associate. She's been working as a cashier for three weeks now, trying to get to know her co-workers. Jenny's been keeping Robert apprised of day-to-day developments, and he's getting antsy about expenses. It costs the production several hundred dollars per day to keep Jenny "embedded," and Robert's wondering if it's time to fish or cut bait.

Feeling the pressure from headquarters, Jenny decides to make a tentative approach to see if two of her co-workers might be willing to cooperate in the film. Planning her next move, Jenny realizes that the mechanics are trickier than she had first thought. If she reveals her true identity to a co-worker, and the co-worker reports her to management, then her cover will be blown and the entire month will have been a waste of time and money.

So Jenny decides to try something different that will preserve her cover. Talking about the documentary inside the store is out of the question, so she meets with one of her fellow Wal-Mart associates in a private home. Jenny tells her fellow cashier about a strange call she's received from Los Angeles. The producers of a documentary film are wondering if she'd be willing to allow a camera crew into her life to see what it's like to work at Wal-Mart.

Her co-worker is astounded. "Now why would you go and do a crazy thing like that? You'll lose your job," she warns. During a different in-home meeting, another of Jenny's co-workers reacts similarly. It's clear to Jenny that these two women are focused on putting bread on the table. The idea of making some kind of social or political statement about Wal-Mart strikes them immediately as self-destructive and pointless.

When Robert hears about this experience, he's ready to pull the plug. So is Jenny. "We would need much more time to build relationships," she says. "Maybe if I could have worked there for six months, I would have fifty co-workers to choose from. I could have stopped working at the store, and then approached my former co-workers as a co-producer of the film."

Even then, the obstacles would have been significant. After six months of filming Wal-Mart stories around the country, Robert's activities would surely have been detected by Wal-Mart management in Bentonville. By that time store managers would be on the lookout for any signs of a filmmaker poking around looking to interview associates.

In evaluating what to do next, Robert weighs evidence gleaned from the activities of his other co-producers. Caty has been using an up-front and honest approach to find a current employee, and has also come up empty. Regardless of

Former Wal-Mart associate Diane Devoy.

the who, where, or how, it's been impossible to secure the cooperation of someone who is currently employed by Wal-Mart. The *Hoop Dreams* method would have required an ongoing camera presence in an associate's life, making that person an undercover agent at Wal-Mart just like Jenny. It's too much to ask of a person who's simply trying to make ends meet.

Robert decides to re-deploy Jenny on the story of Diane Devoy, a former Wal-Mart hourly associate. Other than her former employee status, Diane suits Robert's original crite-

the high cost of low price

ria quite well. She's a single mom, and was receiving public assistance while working at Wal-Mart. Jenny's new mission is to spend some time filming Diane and her family, capturing not only her feelings about working at Wal-Mart but also the texture of her day-to-day life as a member of the working poor.

WAL★MART
the high cost of low price

See the Hub, Be the Hub

Lisa: "It's becoming a pissing contest."
Rick: "Who is pissing on who?"
Lisa: "I think it's who can piss the highest."
Rick: "Is anyone pissing on us?"
Lisa: "I don't think so."
Rick: "So then everyone is playing together nicely, yes?"

Robert's political team is talking. Loudly. Rapidly. Interrupting each other. The discussion ranges across topics, asides, and jokes. When Rick and Lisa get together, it's like a conversational fencing match written by David Mamet.

Lisa Smithline is Robert's political director, and has been coordinating outreach to organizations that are concerned about Wal-Mart. A Jewish mother in dreadlocks and jeans, Lisa's a little artsy, a little crunchy, and a lot intense.

Rick Jacobs is an investment advisor turned party activist, and was Howard Dean's California campaign chair. Known for his fashionably-tailored suits, Rick exudes player status. Now a partner in Brave New Films, Rick's been working the phones trying to raise seed capital from wealthy progressives.

Robert has challenged Lisa and Rick to create the largest grass-roots campaign ever assembled around a documentary film. Robert's dream is to launch the documentary on Sunday, November 13 with anti-Wal-Mart sermons in a thousand churches. The sermons would mark the official beginning of "Wal-Mart Week." Each of the following six days would spotlight a different issue raised by Wal-Mart's business practices, from "Health Care" to "Main Street Shopkeepers" to "Environmental Impact." Viewing parties for the Retail Project would take place across the entire seven days of Wal-Mart Week.

Brave New Films principal Rick Jacobs and political director Lisa Smithline.

The viewing parties would range from small in-home gatherings to larger screenings at community centers and union halls. Environmental groups would help organize viewing parties on Environment Day and union groups would promote viewing parties on Workers' Day. High-school teachers would design lesson plans for Learn About

WAL-MART
the high cost of low price

Wal-Mart Day, and politicians would promote their Wal-Mart-inspired bills on Legislative Action Day. This ambitious plan requires the involvement of a broad coalition of organizations, perhaps even a hundred different groups.

The idea of "Wal-Mart Week" originated with Andrew Stern, the powerful and charismatic president of the Service Employees International Union. Right after Election Day, Stern started a new organization called Wal-Mart Watch, charged with exposing and challenging Wal-Mart's employment practices. Wal-Mart Watch is a joint project of the Center for Community & Corporate Ethics and its advocacy arm, Five Stones. The biblical name references David's modest arsenal in his battle with Goliath.

Shortly after Robert made the decision to move forward with the Retail Project, he was contacted by the SEIU. Stern was going to be in Los Angeles and wanted to have a meeting. In early January, Stern came to Robert's office for a sit-down, along with his deputy Gina Glantz and Andy Grossman, the new executive director of Wal-Mart Watch.

Stern made a big impression on Robert and Lisa. He was fired up about Robert's movie and hungry to find ways to harness the film as a grass-roots organizing tool. Stern explained his idea for "Wal-Mart Week," a seven-day blast of anti-Wal-Mart activity encompassing a wide variety of issues and advocacy groups. Stern told Robert that his movie would be the perfect driver of Wal-Mart Week.

Robert and Lisa were thrilled, and the conversation turned to dates. The week of November 13-19 looked ideal, an opportunity to sour the public mood on Wal-Mart in the final days before the start of the crucial holiday selling season.

Although completing the movie by November 2005 would be a major challenge for Robert and his team, it seemed like the planets were aligning for a high-profile launch. By the end of the meeting, Robert and Stern had agreed to November 13 as the "release date" for the documentary and the launch date for "Wal-Mart Week."

During the first four months of 2005, Rick and Lisa have been working their rolodexes to reach out to any conceivable organization that might want to participate in Wal-Mart Week. The ever-growing list of affiliated organizations makes for some strange bedfellows. The Petroleum Marketers Association of America and the Sierra Club are on opposite sides of almost every issue. Yet the PMAA, representing independently-owned gas stations, opposes Wal-Mart's lowball gasoline pricing, and has decided to get behind Robert's movie.

Assembling this broad coalition is no easy task, and one of the main challenges is figuring out how to keep everyone on the same page. Robert and Lisa's original concept was to use Wal-Mart Watch as the "Hub." Groups that were interested in getting involved in promoting the film could connect to the Retail Project through the Hub, freeing up Robert's staff from the day-to-day management of the grassroots coalition.

Yet Wal-Mart Watch was a brand-new organization that was just getting off the ground. In early 2005, Wal-Mart Watch was staffing up, defining its mission, signing up members, and developing a rapport with the press. In these early days Wal-Mart Watch was functioning primarily as a "rapid response" team, alerting the news media to new Wal-Mart controversies as they arose, and counterspinning the company line whenever possible.

Meanwhile, another union-funded organization, Wake-Up Wal-Mart, was also getting noticed by the press. Wake-Up Wal-Mart is a creation of the United Food and Commercial Workers, who have been attempting to organize Wal-Mart for over a decade. In an effort to revitalize Wake-Up

the high cost of low price

Wal-Mart after the presidential election, the UFCW hired Paul Blank as Wake-Up Wal-Mart's new director. Just twenty-nine years old, Blank had served as political director for the Howard Dean presidential campaign, and promised to bring Deaniacs and their internet-driven techniques into the fold.

Robert and Lisa had not realized during their meeting with Stern that the SEIU was a late entrant in the multi-union pressure campaign against Wal-Mart. Virulently anti-union, and without a single unionized worksite, Wal-Mart had become the biggest problem and yet the biggest prize for the labor movement, and everybody wanted in on the action.

In the spring of 2005, the relationship between the UFCW's "Wake-Up Wal-Mart" and the SEIU's "Wal-Mart Watch" was still evolving. According to a May 2005 article in the *Washington Post*, both Wake-Up Wal-Mart and Wal-Mart Watch have been "trying to build alliances with other groups that disagree with Wal-Mart policies." Describing the relationship between Wake-Up Wal-Mart and Wal-Mart Watch, Liza Featherstone wrote on Salon.com that "there are petty turf wars and rivalries between the two groups, but what's striking is how potentially complementary they are." (Featherstone is the author of a book about the *Dukes* case and gender discrimination at Wal-Mart.)

Yet some of the grass-roots organizations Lisa's been in contact with are not entirely comfortable with operating under the umbrella of either union-backed organization. Certain groups oppose Wal-Mart's impact on small-town main streets. Others resent the company's failure to provide medical insurance to hundreds of thousands of employees, thereby placing an unfair burden on county hospitals and other providers of health care to the uninsured. Still other groups are primarily focused on the environment, on overseas sweatshop labor, or on the economic health of local businesses. Each of these groups has different objectives, different action plans, and different political leanings.

The goal for today's meeting in early May is for Lisa and Rick to figure out how to get all of these groups pulling in the same direction. Over the last few months, there's been a lot of enthusiasm for the Retail Project in this constellation of organizations, but Lisa and Rick have had a hard time getting organizations to commit to a fixed timetable of concrete actions to promote the film.

As the meeting draws to a close, Lisa recaps Robert's original goal for the film. He has said that the Retail Project should be a "tool" for the various organizations, each to use in their own way. He often says his film itself will not change Wal-Mart, but perhaps it will inspire people and organizations to force change upon the massive company.

A veteran of progressive grass-roots organizing, Lisa's always been skeptical of top-down, command-and-control structures. She's never wanted Brave New Films to direct the movement; from the beginning, Lisa and Robert have wanted the film to help the movement attract new supporters and become stronger and better-organized on its own.

A rebel at heart, Lisa's naturally biased in favor of loose coordination and individual autonomy. Yet the marketing campaign for a film cannot be loosely organized. Although Robert's unorthodox techniques are completely different than the way a major studio would release a film, everything still depends on building excitement towards a high-profile launch. And a high profile launch requires advance planning, tight coordination, and a fixed timetable for the rollout.

Wary of trying to organize a movement, Rick and Lisa still need to organize a marketing campaign, which in this case means convening thousands of house-parties during Wal-Mart Week. And with the public announcement of the

the high cost of low price

Retail Project just a month away, a number of key decisions need to be made quickly.

Will the Retail Project coordinate the house parties, or will each organization handle that for their own members? Regarding sales of the DVD, what will be the economic relationship between the organizations and the Retail Project? Will organizations order bulk copies of the DVD and resell them to their members? Or will the organizations simply refer interested members to the Retail Project site and then receive a commission on each sale?

As Rick stands up and prepares to leave, there's a pregnant pause in the rapid-fire conversation. On his way out of Lisa's office, Rick turns to her and asks with trepidation, "Soooo, from now on, are we the Hub?"

"Yes, I think we're the Hub," she replies, "at least for the time being."

WAL★MART
the high cost of low price

Behind Enemy Lines

In early May, Caty and Kristy are wrapping up a three-day stint in Lumberton, North Carolina, the first stop of a fifteen-day trip. Over the past six weeks, they've become good friends, flying, driving, shooting, schlepping, and commiserating together.

Four days ago, Caty made her first attempt at handling sound duties in addition to her role as co-producer. Initially, Caty was intimidated by her lack of experience with sound equipment, but she's found that wearing headphones has helped her become more conscious of what's actually being captured on tape. Liberated from watching the audio levels, Kristy is now free to put all her attention into the visuals, which is a great help in wielding her hand-held camera. By taking on sound duties, Caty's enabled the production to realize the benefits of improved sound quality without the incremental cost of adding a third crew member.

Beyond the mechanics of shooting, Caty and Kristy have also been honing their personal approach with the people they meet. Walking down small-town Main streets dressed casually in jeans and baseball caps, they are often mistaken for college students. Fresh faced, pretty, and cheerful, Caty and Kristy present themselves as warm, sincere, and non-threatening. Rather than trying to impress people with the scope of Robert's investigative effort, Caty and Kristy have perfected a low-key approach, soft-pedaling the size of the crew that's toiling back in Culver City.

In Lumberton, Caty and Kristy have been shooting interviews with former Wal-Mart associates. Like Jenny, Caty's been striking out on the urgent goal of finding current Wal-Mart employees who will cooperate with the film. Former Wal-Mart employees, however, seem to be more than happy to air their frustrations and disappointments on camera.

On the way out of Lumberton, Caty and Kristy are excited yet anxious about their next stop. After several months of gathering Wal-Mart stories in small-town America, they are now heading right for the mothership itself, Wal-Mart's corporate headquarters in Bentonville, Arkansas.

At this point Robert has not made any contact with the Wal-Mart corporation, preferring to fly under the radar for a bit longer before asking upper management to sit for an interview. Yet Robert's hoping that Bentonville itself can be a great source for evocative B-roll that can attach a sense of place to the company and its management.

On the evening of May 5, Caty and Kristy board a tiny commuter plane heading to Fayetteville, Arkansas. There are only twenty people on the flight, and everyone's in business attire except Caty and Kristy, who are wearing jeans. As soon as they sit down, Caty and Kristy overhear businessmen in the row ahead of them talking about a deal they are doing with Wal-Mart. Picking up other fragments of conversations from around the plane, Caty and Kristy get the feeling that they are the only people on board who don't

the high cost of low price

work for or sell to Wal-Mart. It truly feels like a trip behind enemy lines.

Once in the privacy of their rental car, Caty and Kristy compare notes on the experience. "We're going to be right under their noses, filming everything we can," exclaims Caty, feeling a bit of bravado—but there's an undercurrent of fear, as well. Exactly what will it be like tomorrow, operating in the belly of the beast? Does Wal-Mart have such an iron grip on their home turf that outsiders poking around with a camera will be detected, possibly even surveiled?

Checking into their hotel a few hours later, Caty asks the front desk clerk for ideas on where to buy some food, bottled water, and other provisions for their stay. "There's a Wal-Mart a few miles north, and another Wal-Mart a little bit further south," he says. "There's another Wal-Mart down the road to the east." Reluctant to spend their money with the megacorporation, Kristy asks if there are any independent supermarkets in the area. "Nah, pretty much all roads lead to Wal-Mart," he replies.

The next morning, Caty and Kristy head over to Wal-Mart's corporate headquarters to scope out the territory. At first they are cautious, wary of the security cameras in the parking lot. Yet a tremendous number of people seem to be coming and going. Rather than having a small-town feeling, Bentonville seems like a boomtown, clogged with rental cars, hotel guests, and construction sites. Hundreds of people who appear to be out-of-towners are entering and leaving Wal-Mart's offices, and gradually Caty and Kristy feel less conspicuous.

It's time to do some filming. Caty parks the car across the street from the main Wal-Mart office building, and Kristy readies the camera low in the car where it can't be seen by passersby. When Kristy's all set to roll tape, Caty puts the car in drive and lightly places her foot on the gas pedal, ready to pull out at the slightest sign of a problem.

But there's no problem. Kristy takes her time and gets all the B-roll she needs, shooting through the open window of the rental car.

Feeling emboldened, Caty and Kristy decide their next stop is the private residence of Wal-Mart CEO Lee Scott. Surely there'll be a place in the film for an image of Scott's mansion. The only problem is finding his mansion. He's probably not listed in the white pages.

Caty's heard that many of Wal-Mart's heavy hitters live in a gated, golf-course community called the Pinnacle, which is located in the neighboring town of Rogers. Caty drives to Rogers, in the hopes that somehow they can find Scott's house. Passing a FedEx office, Caty and Kristy decide to go inside seeking more info. "We're looking for Lee Scott's house," they chirp, two friendly young ladies with big smiles. "That's easy, it's inside a gated community," replies the man behind the counter, and he promptly tells Caty the exact street address.

"We were hoping to take a picture standing in front of his house," explains Caty. "Is there any way we could get in?"

"Tell the guard that you're coming to have lunch with Mrs. Robinson at the country club, and he'll probably let you right in," says the helpful FedEx man, and Robert's dynamic duo of investigators jump in the car and do exactly that.

Successfully inside the Pinnacle, Kristy starts shooting the houses as Caty drives slowly along a street called Wimbledon. The houses are new and huge, occupying almost all of each piece of land. "It feels like the backlot of a studio," Caty remarks. "I guess when you're a big Wal-Mart executive, you live within the company twenty-four/seven. Your co-workers are your golf buddies, your travel buddies, and your neighbors."

the high cost of low price

In fact, the Rogers area is nationally-known amongst real-estate professionals as one of the fastest-growing zip-codes in the country. The increased affluence of Wal-Mart's managers has coincided with an influx of Fortune 500 executives coming to Bentonville to manage their "customer relationship" with the world's largest retailer.

Demand for upscale goods and services in Rogers is exploding. Near the gated community there are the "Shoppes at Pinnacle Hills" and a gourmet supermarket. Apparently the hotel concierge was wrong. There is somewhere to buy food other than the Wal-Mart superstore, conveniently located for Wal-Mart's own top executives to do their high-end shopping. There's also Pinnacle Air Services, offering charter flights on three private jets.

The conspicuous consumption of Pinnacle Hills stands in sharp contrast to the corporate culture of Wal-Mart under founder Sam Walton. Company lore is filled with stories of Sam's constant vigilance against wasteful spending and ostentatious display of wealth. Legend has it that Sam would even troll through the company parking lot, ready to admonish anyone bold enough to drive to work in a flashy, expensive car.

With a second day of B-roll shooting planned for tomorrow, Caty's looking forward to the day after, when former Wal-Mart store manager Jon Lehman flies into Bentonville for an interview. Jon is the first former manager to agree to appear on camera, and Caty plans to ask him about a number of Wal-Mart's controversial business practices. Having grown up in Arkansas, Lehman also has a wealth of knowledge about the Walton family and the early days of Wal-Mart, and has promised to take Caty and Kristy to the site of the family's hardened underground security bunker.

On the morning of May 8, Lehman arrives in town for his interview. It's raining, and Kristy's worried. The plan is to interview Lehman outdoors at a variety of significant sites in and around Bentonville, and he's booked on a flight out of town at the end of the day. There are only eight hours to shoot Lehman, and the loss of Bentonville's visual flavor will be significant.

Yet luck is not with Caty and Kristy on this particular day. It rains and rains. The only choice other than shooting Lehman in a generic hotel room is conducting the interviews in his rental car. So Kristy sets up shop in the passenger seat to film Jon talking about Wal-Mart as he drives around the town. Caty works through a variety of questions and topics, gathering information for Robert's investigation. As the interview unfolds, it becomes clear that Jon's greatest value may be his ability to confirm the systemic nature of many Wal-Mart misdeeds, actions that CEO Lee Scott says are rare breaches of company policy by a small number of overzealous "knuckleheads."

Former Wal-Mart store manager Jon Lehman.

Later that night, Caty tells Kristy that she's hoping to find another former Wal-Mart manager to complement today's interview. "It would be great to talk to someone who can speak to the emotional toll of doing that job," Caty says. If such a person can be found, it won't be in Bentonville, because Caty and Kristy are leaving town tomorrow, heading back to North Carolina for three more days of shooting.

WAL-MART
the high cost of low price

☺ Changing Plans

On the very same day that Caty and Kristy interview Lehman, a Sam's Club employee in Gastonia, North Carolina, posts a brief comment on the Wake-Up Wal-Mart blog. Her nine-sentence plea for help mentions "discrimination," "harassment," and "violations of my union activity." She's looking for an attorney who can help her with the Equal Opportunity Employment Commission. Her name is Beverly Ingle, and the post includes her phone number and e-mail address.

Beverly doesn't know about the Retail Project, and the Retail Project doesn't know about Beverly. Not yet.

Back at the Culver City headquarters, Robert is feeling acute deadline pressure, and passing that pressure on to the staff. He opens the May 10 weekly staff meeting with an announcement. "The next four to five weeks I will be driving everyone to collect a ton of footage. Once we get into June," he warns, "it becomes harder for the editors to plug in new stuff. I want to be able to watch a first assembly of the entire film before July 1."

The next day, Robert hammers the point home with an e-mail entitled "State of the State of the Film." Sent to the entire staff, the e-mail pinpoints three equally-important priorities for the researchers and co-producers.

First, Robert's honing in on the subsidies Wal-Mart often receives from local governments. He's looking for shopkeepers, government officials, first-responders, and teachers who can talk about the taxpayer money that flows to Wal-Mart from local and county governments, money that is often raised from taxes on the existing local businesses. "I want to find a story where the closing of a family-run business is tied directly to a corporate subsidy received by Wal-Mart," he tells the staff. "The goal is to help the audience see, feel, and comprehend the human toll of a complex and hard-to-understand form of corporate welfare."

Robert's second priority is crime, specifically crime committed in Wal-Mart parking lots. Internet researcher Meleiza has found dozens of high-profile local cases in which Wal-Mart's customers and associates have been assaulted and even abducted from Wal-Mart parking lots. Some of these crime victims have sued the company for providing inadequate security. Meleiza's been passing her leads on to video researcher Jaffar Mahmood, who digs for local television news footage about these crimes. Jaffar's stack of crime clips is growing, and Robert wants the co-producers to find a few of these victims who would be willing to talk on camera about their experiences.

The final priority is the continuing search for the current employee. Robert has expanded this quest to include former Wal-Mart employees as well. The paragraph in his e-mail about this topic concludes with a sentence that's written in capital letters. "EVERYONE ON ALERT FOR THIS. PASS ALONG LEADS TO CATY + JENNY WHEN WE FIND THEM."

the high cost of low price

Following his own directive, Robert asks Meleiza if she happens to have any new leads for Caty and Kristy, who are in North Carolina for the next few days. "As a matter of fact, I think I do," Meleiza replies, telling Robert about a disgruntled Sam's Club employee who posted her 704 area code phone number on the Wake-Up Wal-Mart blog a few days ago. "E-mail me the information and I'll pass it along to Caty," Robert says.

Filmmaker's Toolbox: Obtaining News Clips

All three of Robert Greenwald's documentaries rely heavily on archival news clips. Yet each film presented unique problems for Robert's research team. On *Uncovered*, Jim Gilliam developed a method to transfer C-Span's streaming videoclips from his computer to VHS tape. This technique enabled the editors to work with the Bush administration's public statements just days after they aired. One reviewer called *Uncovered* an "insta-doc" because of its rapid-response rebuttal of the government.

Outfoxed was focused on capturing and analyzing the broadcasts of a single network: Fox News Channel. Robert's team developed a rack of DVD recorders that could automatically capture the entire Fox News daily broadcast. As one DVD recorder ran out of disc space, another unit automatically started recording, creating a complete twenty-four/seven archive.

The Retail Project presents a completely different challenge in terms of archival footage. Covering community-based stories from all over the country, the film requires local rather than national news footage, and sometimes the stories date back a year or two.

Footage researcher Jaffar Mahmood explains his technique:

My first step is to call the local television station that covered the story. Very few local stations actually record and archive their own broadcasts. Usually stations refer you to a local mom-and-pop company that records local newscasts and sells VHS tapes of particular clips. Most of these monitoring companies only keep news reports on tape for 30-90 days, because the bulk of their business comes from viewers who want a personal copy of something they recently saw on TV.

As the "Riverkeeper" story was coming together in April, Robert told me that a particular clip from a local North Carolina station was an absolute "must-have." The story aired in 2002, and was the turning point in Donna Lisenbee's campaign to pressure Wal-Mart to stop polluting the Catawba River. I hit countless brick walls tracking down the clip, and asked Jim for advice. Jim advised me to call Multivision, a national monitoring company who had already told me they only keep North Carolina stories on file for 90 days.

Jim smiled and said, "you gotta call back and say 'I'll pay anything necessary to get this clip.'" So I

the high cost of low price

*called back, said the magic words, and was put
on hold. The woman finally came back on the line,
took my credit card information, and a day later
we had the clip in hand for less than $300. Who
says money can't solve your problems?*

Of course, obtaining the footage itself is the easy part.
Getting the legal rights to include a clip in the film is
a wholly separate endeavor, which begins when the
director has a pretty solid rough cut and knows what
material is likely to make the final version.

Caty and Kristy already have three full days of shooting
in the Charlotte area scheduled for May 10-12, with tickets
to fly home on May 13. As currently planned, they would
not have enough time to interview someone new on this
trip. But it's certainly worth making a phone call.

On May 11, Caty makes her first call to Beverly Ingle, three days after Beverly posted on the Wake-Up Wal-
Mart blog. Beverly is happy to hear from Caty, delighted
that someone actually noticed her blog post. Since Beverly
seems interested in cooperating with the film, Caty moves
into "pre-interview" mode, hoping to find out as much as
possible. During the conversation, Beverly tells Caty about a
friend, Kathy Nicholson, who formerly worked at Wal-Mart.
Her husband used to be one of the managers Wal-Mart
would fly around the country to stores in which union activity was detected. Caty's ears prick up. "Can I have their
number?" she asks. "Sure," says Beverly, "it's Cathy and
Wheldon Nicholson. They live right here in Gastonia."

Caty's next call is to Robert, briefing him on Beverly
and the Nicholsons. "I'm wondering if this Wheldon guy

could be even more interesting than Beverly or Kathy," Robert muses aloud. "That's exactly what I'm thinking," Caty replies. "May I extend the trip for one or two more days to try to get Beverly and Wheldon on tape?" "Absolutely," Robert responds.

On May 13, Caty and Kristy eat breakfast with Wheldon at a local diner. On the phone the day before, Wheldon told Caty he wasn't willing to go on camera. Caty convinced him that meeting in person and chatting about the film over breakfast couldn't hurt.

The breakfast goes well, and by the time the waitress brings the check, Wheldon is game. "I've never had a chance to speak about this," he tells Caty. "Maybe it will give me a chance to reclaim my soul."

After a quick interview at Beverly's house, Caty and Kristy head over to the Nicholsons and end up staying the afternoon, shooting almost three hours of footage. Sitting on a couch in his dimly-lit living room, Wheldon takes Caty, Kristy, and the camera on a dark tour through his seventeen years as a Wal-Mart manager. The room becomes a confessional, and the camera becomes Wheldon's priest.

Wheldon's story unfolds like a Greek tragedy, full of treachery, hubris, and regret. Referring to himself as a "good soldier," Wheldon talks about having to relearn how to be a caring person at the end of seventeen years inside the company. The work Wheldon did

Former Wal-Mart store manager Wheldon Nicholson.

for Wal-Mart has affected him the way combat can cause post-traumatic stress disorder in a war veteran.

And he describes his dirty work in explicit detail. Shav-

ing hours from employee paychecks. Manipulating department managers to work "off the clock." Terminating associates for even the slightest sign of union activity. Using illegal immigrants as overnight janitors. Having worked in many stores in several states, Wheldon claims these activities took place in every location he worked, and are part of an unwritten code shared by Wal-Mart managers.

Caty and Kristy can't believe their ears. The interview is pure gold, a major break in Robert's five-month investigation of the world's largest corporation.

Returning home to Los Angeles, Caty and Kristy arrive at the May 17 staff meeting in a bubbly, even triumphant mood. Their big smiles indicate more than just being happy to see their colleagues again after two long weeks on the road. "It feels like everything we shot is going to be in the movie," Caty gushes to one of the producers, as the staff files into Robert's office. Caty hands the Wheldon tape to Robert, who asks the assistant editors to digitize and transcribe the material immediately.

The room quiets down, and Robert begins the meeting with a bombshell: He's officially abandoning the *Hoop Dreams* concept. Robert has reluctantly yet decisively concluded that the current employee "A-story" is not obtainable. The experience of life as a Wal-Mart employee will instead be explored by soundbites from a variety of former Wal-Mart associates and managers.

This change necessitates a radical shift in the structure of the film. Rather than an A-story featuring the main character interspersed with a variety of B-stories, the new structure will have at least a dozen primary characters, each of whom will star in their own segment.

"The new model is *The Towering Inferno*," exclaims Robert with a grin. "Terrible movie, great structure. You introduce the characters of your ensemble cast in the first reel.

Then the disaster happens, and we see how each of the characters deal with it. It's now a disaster movie, and Wal-Mart is the disaster!"

Robert's tone hardens, as he warns the staff once again that the bulk of the filming needs to be completed by mid-June. "We're moving into serious crunchtime," he says. "Our big challenge is to fill out some of the substantive areas of the film. The next five weeks are going to be crucial."

the high cost of low price

☺ Inglewood

Co-producer Kerry Candaele and his cameraman Mobo-laji Olambiwonnu are filming interviews at a middle-school softball game in Inglewood, California on Memorial Day weekend. The small baseball diamond is in Darby Park, perched atop a hill that's four miles east of the Los Angeles International Airport. Just downhill from home plate is the edge of the vast deserted parking lot that surrounds the Hollywood Park horse track.

Robert is especially excited about the Inglewood story. Back in 2003, Wal-Mart proposed building a new Supercenter on sixty acres of the Hollywood Park land. Encountering resistance from the Inglewood City Council, Wal-Mart decided to take their development plan directly to the voters in a special election. After spending over a million dollars in support of their ballot initiative, Wal-Mart got just 4,575 votes, versus 7,049 votes against the superstore. Wal-Mart's loss at the ballot box became a very public defeat, as the story was covered by newspapers around the world. Robert sees

Inglewood's resistance movement as one of the rare "success stories" that can end his film on an inspiring note.

Another reason Robert is so fired up about Inglewood is that the segment features one of his most compelling characters, the Reverend Altagracia Perez. Articulate, passionate, and beautiful, Perez is a powerful advocate for communities taking control of their own economic destiny. There's a wide selection of great Perez footage, including her sermon marking the one-year anniversary of Wal-Mart's ballot defeat, a discussion of Inglewood politics while cooking spaghetti sauce in her kitchen, and her visit to Bentonville to lobby Wal-Mart's management.

The Bentonville footage includes a comment from Perez in which she describes how Wal-Mart expects everyone they deal with to be as docile as the company's suppliers. "They are used to sitting in those little boxes with the windows and knocking everybody down to what they want. In a negotiation they always win," she explains. Perez sees the Inglewood victory as proof that you can stand up to Wal-Mart.

Doug Cheek spent a good portion of April editing the Inglewood footage, whittling it down to a ten-minute segment which Robert viewed in early May. Although the Inglewood "site fight" took place a year before the Retail Project got underway, there's plenty of local news footage available to tell the story. Intercutting the news footage with Perez's personal narrative has been very effective, and Robert is thrilled with the results. The one thing still missing is some good B-roll that can establish the Inglewood community and be used for cutaways.

Kerry and Mobolaji are in Darby Park today in search of the footage necessary to complete the Inglewood segment. The baseball diamond where they are shooting is a difficult environment for audio, because of the planes flying over-

the high cost of low price

head. Inglewood, population 112,000, is located directly beneath the final approach for planes arriving at LAX.

Darby Park is almost exactly in between the two parallel flight paths, so it's jumbo jet in stereo. Planes roar overhead at two-minute intervals, necessitating a talk-pause-talk-pause conversational rhythm. It seems the interviewees are interrupted almost every time they get started on a thought or a story. One of them tells us that Inglewood residents are well-versed at "riding the volume button on the remote control" while watching television.

Mobolaji, an assistant editor doing double-duty as camera operator, suggests moving indoors, but Kerry says that would be too boring. Kerry is mindful of Robert's constant pressure to film people in their natural environment, "doing something." (One of the early goals Robert established with Kristy was to capture the texture of everyday life as much as possible. Thus far, interviewees have been filmed doing a wide variety of household tasks including raking the lawn, folding laundry and making a scrapbook.)

Assistant editor Mobolaji Olambiwonnu shooting in Inglewood, California.

One of Kerry's interviewees is the coach of the softball team, a former Inglewood city councilman who was active in the site fight. Inglewood is a proud island of self-governance in the middle of sprawling Los Angeles County. The city of 9.2 square miles has its own town hall and school system, offering residents a far greater degree of local control than what's available to residents of the City of Angels.

Although Hispanics have been moving into the west side of Inglewood at a rapid rate, city politics remain largely an African-American affair. The longtime social and political anchor of the community is an area called the "Avenues," streets of single-family detached homes owned by middle class African-American families. The Avenues used to be famous for an annual Christmas-lights bonanza in which entire blocks would put forth amazing displays of holiday decoration. Angelenos from across the region used to drive through the Avenues every December to admire the festive scenery.

According to the 2000 census, there are almost 11,000 single-family, owner-occupied homes in Inglewood. The median household income is a little over $34,000, and twenty-two percent of residents fall below the poverty level. Less than fourteen percent of residents have a bachelor's degree or higher.

In other words, Inglewood is a stable, working-class community. The constant roar of planes limits the potential for gentrification, and the solid base of unionized jobs at the airport and other nearby places provides a sustainable income for non-college-educated workers.

Sylvia Hopper is one of these workers. She's been at Lucky Stores for almost thirty years. Sylvia started at Lucky as a teenage bagger, and has worked her way up to a bookkeeping position. She comes from a "proud union family," and is a UFCW shop steward. During her interview with Kerry, Sylvia explains that the union wages and benefits at Lucky have enabled her and her husband to become homeowners and pursue the American dream. There are five

the high cost of low price

unionized grocery stores in Inglewood, and according to Sylvia these stores are an important part of Inglewood's economic self-sufficiency.

Although Wal-Mart has not yet reached critical mass in Southern California, the company's 2002 announcement of plans to build up to forty California Supercenters was enough to cause an earthquake in the grocery business. The established grocery chains, all unionized, decided they could not compete with Wal-Mart in the future without radically restructuring their labor costs. The result was a bitter four-and-a-half-month lockout that affected almost everyone who shopped for food in Los Angeles County. During the strike, simply picking up a quart of milk on the way home from work became a political act, raising awareness of economic and labor issues in a way that no rally or speech ever could.

The grocery strike was settled on February 29, 2004, less than six weeks before Inglewood voted on Wal-Mart's development plan. The economic empowerment argument made by Sylvia and hundreds of local workers was powerfully illustrated by the supermarket strike and resonated with Inglewood's voters.

Sylvia is being interviewed while sitting on the grass, with her back to the Hollywood Park Racetrack's small dirt practice ring. In an attempt to juice up fading revenues from horse racing, the Hollywood Park Operating Company opened a casino at the racetrack in 1994, and then sold the entire property for $140 million to Churchill Downs Incorporated in 1999. The management of Churchill Downs, who operate the famous Kentucky Derby, hoped to revitalize Hollywood Park's horse-racing operations. After a few years of experience in Inglewood, Churchill Downs figured out that the land underneath Hollywood Park Racetrack was more valuable than the racetrack itself. Much more valuable.

Hollywood Park and the surrounding parking lots once measured almost 300 acres. As "infill" development became more and more popular with big real-estate companies, the price-per-acre of this huge site continued to rise.

The proposed Wal-Mart development would be the third major parcel of Hollywood Park's property to be broken off and developed. A gated community of new single-family homes called "Renaissance" is rising on the east edge of the Hollywood Park Property, at the foot of the hill on which Sylvia is perched. While Mobolaji resets the camera, Sylvia marvels at the $400,000 prices being asked for these new homes that will be overflown by jetliners around the clock. Apparently there is a huge waiting list for the homes at Renaissance, which are some of the first new houses to be built in Inglewood in decades.

Another parcel of the Hollywood Park property has already been turned into a big-box shopping area, including national retailers Target, Home Depot, Walgreen's, Bally's Total Fitness, and Starbucks. In April of 2005, Inglewood's mayor Roosevelt Dorn predicted that the remaining 238 acres of Hollywood Park could be sold for as much as $250 million. (On July 7, 2005, Churchill Downs announced an agreement to sell Hollywood Park Racetrack and the surrounding land to a private real-estate fund for $260 million.)

After Wal-Mart's first Supercenter proposal was defeated at the ballot box in April 2004, the company, its developer, or a related entity purchased the sixty acres of land on which their store would have been built, suggesting that the "site fight" is nowhere near over. Inglewood's activists have responded with a public relations campaign to force Wal-Mart to radically revise their next proposal.

Sylvia Hopper and Reverend Perez are two of the signatories of an April 5, 2005 letter to Wal-Mart CEO Lee Scott. The letter, from the Coalition for a Better Inglewood, demands

the high cost of low price

that Wal-Mart sign a Community Benefits Agreement with the City of Inglewood as a precondition for building a Supercenter. The proposed agreement would "guarantee living wage jobs, affordable family health care, fair pension benefits, job training and advancement, freedom from retaliation, and basic rights on the job. It will also protect the interests of small businesses, and ensure that your project does not increase crime, traffic, noise, and pollution in our city."

An agreement of this type would represent a top-to-bottom rethink of Wal-Mart's business model. Is demanding a Community Benefits Agreement a viable strategy for Inglewood and other communities? And will Robert's movie be able to raise these kind of big-picture questions in a ten-minute-or-less segment about the Inglewood site-fight?

Back at HQ two weeks later, Doug is reviewing the Inglewood footage and scowling. "I asked for B-roll, not new characters," he moans. "I've got all the talkers I need for this segment! All I wanted was some generic shots of life in the community."

Of the hours of new tape submitted by Kerry and Mobolaji, the only clip that interests Doug is a brief shot of a father and son skateboarding together, the son riding on his father's shoulders. The duo rounds a corner from the small businesses of Inglewood's commercial district to a leafy residential street. In this five-second clip, Doug sees a window into the spirit of Inglewood.

According to Doug, when the co-producers return to the scene of a previous shoot, they often do not deliver the supplementary footage the editors have requested. "It happens all the time," he says. It seems that Kerry has ignored Doug's "shot list," in favor of continuing to explore Inglewood's citizen resistance to corporate power.

WAL*MART
the high cost of low price

😊 Money, Time, and the *Times*

A large sum of production funds arrived today. Few people know, and those who do aren't celebrating.

Around three in the afternoon, producer Devin Smith heard from the bank that wire transfers from the first two investors in Brave New Films had arrived. Devin immediately walked through the courtyard to give Robert the good news in person.

For the last six months, Robert has been personally funding the Retail Project, while Rick Jacobs has been on a long and difficult search to find individual investors. Robert is used to having the money people eventually catch on to his ideas. Robert self-funded *Outfoxed* and *Uncovered*, digging deep into his pockets and even taking out loans to cover production expenses. On both projects, Robert found backers mid-stream and was able to recover his personal investment.

The Retail Project, however, is a larger and more complex production, and costs have been rising rapidly. Currently budgeted at $1.6 million, the film will cost at least three times more to produce than *Outfoxed*. And it's very possible the budget will need to be further increased when the pace of editing picks up later this summer. Several of Rick's potential investors who made their money in entertainment bailed out when faced with the reality of opposing Wal-Mart. The first two investors to actually take the plunge have decided to do so anonymously.

Robert doesn't seem particularly moved or relieved by Devin's good news that approximately two-thirds of the production budget is now in the bank. "We were behind, and we're still behind," Robert says with a strained smile. It's not clear if he's talking about money or time. While Robert rarely speaks to the crew about money matters, lately he's been worrying out loud about running out of time.

Wal-Mart Week is scheduled to begin on November 13, and that date is written in stone. It's the last opportunity to launch the project before Thanksgiving and the holiday season that follows. Right now, the goal is to lock picture by Labor Day, meaning that all creative decisions and editing must be completed by that date.

Earlier this afternoon during the weekly staff meeting, Robert asked the producers to develop scenarios that would buy more time for shooting and editing. Jim Gilliam was resistant. "You should be asking us to push it back a week or two before the deadline, not now," he exclaimed. "You've got months and months left to finish it!"

A hush descended over the room, as the crew waited for Robert's response. "Well, with the size of this one..." Robert paused. "We'll take this up in a smaller meeting," he concluded.

A smaller meeting does indeed convene the next day, but the subject is not the production crunch. It's the title of the movie.

Robert has given an exclusive interview to the *New York*

Times, who will be breaking the story on June 1. The *Times* story will serve as the official announcement that Robert is making a film about Wal-Mart. The reporter wants to know the name of the film, and Robert has to tell him in the next few days.

Robert's working title for the film has been "Wal-Mart: The High Cost of Low Price." In today's meeting, Robert's political and marketing team of Rick, Jim, and Lisa want to take one final look at this title, to make sure it's ready for prime-time. Also attending the meeting are omnipresent co-producer Sarah Feeley and Kabira Stokes, newly hired to help Lisa with grass-roots organizing,

The group discussion begins with the movie title but quickly becomes broader. What is our message at this early stage? How might Wal-Mart counter our message? What's the best way to explain the film's purpose when dealing with the media?

Jim feels that provoking a reaction from Wal-Mart is crucial. "We need to draw fire, which will generate more media attention," he says, speaking like a platoon commander planning to take the next hill.

Refocusing on the movie title itself, the group ponders the implications of incorporating the words "Low Price." Does the title reinforce Wal-Mart's carefully-managed image? Is it wise or foolish to take aim at the very heart of the company's sales pitch?

The group bandies about a variety of alternate titles. Nothing sticks. Robert is not in the room, and it's clear that any title generated here would need solid support from the entire group in order to have a decent shot with Robert.

The meeting breaks, and the working title is still "Wal-Mart: The High Cost of Low Price."

No matter what name the film goes by, the project is about to shift from a private endeavor to a very public one.

Seven days from now, when the *Times* story breaks, you can bet that each and every Wal-Mart employee will be aware of Robert and his film-in-progress.

Up until now, the co-producers have had the ability to operate subtly, disclosing themselves selectively to only those folks who are most likely to be sympathetic to the cause. Once the first wave of publicity hits, the co-producers will be operating in an unpredictable environment where many of the people they encounter could have strong feelings about the film based on the media coverage.

Nobody can predict if the "outing" of the project will make it easier or harder to complete the remaining interviews. Publicity about the Retail Project could make certain people less willing to talk, but it might bring new people to Robert's doorstep. Surely the Bentonville headquarters, which is said to determine the temperature of each and every Wal-Mart store via remote control, will be issuing nationwide directives on how to handle Robert's producers and researchers whenever and wherever they appear.

Another risk is that local news stations may be less willing to license clips to the Retail Project once they know exactly what the film is about. Antagonizing a major advertiser like Wal-Mart isn't exactly at the top of a station manager's to-do list. News footage being one of Robert's favorite storytelling devices, he's pressing the producers to complete licensing the most important clips in the final days before the *Times* article hits.

The afternoon of May 31, we're at T-5, meaning five hours remain before the story about the Retail Project goes up on the *New York Times* website. There's a mood of quiet anticipation at mission control. Everything has been planned and now the team waits to see what will happen when Wal-Mart and the world find out about Robert's new film.

The film's website, WalMartMovie.com, has been com-

the high cost of low price

pleted and is ready to go live at the same moment as the *Times* article is posted. Over the past few weeks, the site, designed by North Carolina webslinger Jesse Haff, has grown larger and more revealing.

Even today, there's some last-minute discussion between Jim, Lisa, and Rick about what level of detail should appear on the website. Jim is focused on creating an initial burst of interest with the media and the general public, while leaving enough mystery so that new information can be revealed in September to add fuel to the fire. On the other hand, Lisa and Rick need materials with a lot more detail in order to convince nonprofits and advocacy organizations to come on board and support the film.

Jim's concept mirrors the traditional way that "event" movies are marketed in Hollywood. About six months before release date, studios run a "teaser trailer" that lets viewers know the movie is coming. The teaser trailer usually has no footage from the actual film; that is saved for trailers that appear much closer to the film's release date.

The trailer that will be viewable at WalMartMovie.com is a teaser trailer. It contains no footage from the film and reveals little about the nature of Robert's critique of Wal-Mart and the company's practices.

Rick, Lisa, and Kabira have access to a much more extensive trailer that does include footage from the film. They've been showing this extended trailer in their meetings with organizations that are considering joining the grass-roots campaign of Wal-Mart Week. In the next few days, this longer trailer will also be the featured attraction at dozens of local meetings organized by Democracy for America, the successor organization to Howard Dean's 2004 presidential campaign. The hope is to generate enthusiasm among former "Deaniacs," enlisting them to spread the word and begin planning house parties to show the film in November.

Originally, Robert and his producers had planned for a fistful of organizations to send e-mails about the Wal-Mart movie to their members at midnight tonight, to maximize the excitement generated by the *New York Times* article. Co-ordinating simultaneous action by these various organizations has proved more difficult than expected.

"This is the first time we've actually asked the partner organizations to do something tangible," explains Jim. "Up to now, we've just been telling them about the project and trying to generate excitement."

"It's been a 'trust me' pitch, to some extent," adds Lisa. "We remind people of what was accomplished with *Out-foxed*, and tell them what a big deal our movie is going to be. I'm hoping that the publicity generated this week will be a way to turn up the heat, *showing* our partners what we're going to accomplish together rather than just telling them."

Filmmaker's Toolbox:
Reaching Out to Organizations

Documentary filmmakers and grass-roots activists have been working together for decades, organizing community screenings to engage the mind and the heart with the storytelling power of film. As early as the 1920s, political films that were rejected by government-controlled theaters in Britain were exhibited by socialist film societies on factory walls and in church social halls. In the 1970s and 80s, documentaries with antiwar, labor, and feminist themes were often shunned by traditional distribution companies in the US and were forced to find alternate means of getting seen, to varying degrees of success. In 1988, filmmaker Barbara Trent reached a large number of people with *Coverup: Behind the*

the high cost of low price

Iran-Contra Affair, using a multi-channel self-distribution strategy that included local activist groups, high-profile benefit screenings at art house theaters, and mail-order distribution on VHS.

As global culture shifts towards the visual and away from the written word, there's an even greater need for visual expression of political ideas. *Outfoxed* and *Uncovered* have demonstrated how digital technology and the internet can offer new ways to find an audience and motivate social change. Yet connecting the dots between political documentaries and the groups that can use them is a difficult and time-consuming task. According to Robert's political director, Lisa Smithline, "many organizers and organizations are not yet familiar with using a film as an organizing tool. Often, my first step is to explain that, as filmmakers, we are trying to provide a useful tool to organizations, adding to their resources instead of taxing their resources."

From the other side of the equation, Gina Glantz of the SEIU sees film as a very powerful and exciting addition to the activist's arsenal. "Inviting people to spend an evening watching a movie is a lot more enticing than inviting them to a lecture or a group discussion," she explains. "And then the movie itself can make abstract issues more tangible, showing the impact of ideas and policies on real people."

In planning their outreach to organizations for the Retail Project, Lisa and Kabira conducted an extensive research project to compile a master list of potential partners. "First we created issue categories relevant to the film," Lisa explains. "Then we searched for as many organizations we could find who were working on those issues. We complied all the information into an Excel spreadsheet so that we could track the status of our discussions with each group."

Before outreach could begin, Lisa needed to assemble materials that could be used to follow up the initial call. While many of today's filmmakers will use a website with a downloadable clip as their main "calling card," Robert's films are usually kept confidential during the first part of the production process. Until the public launch of the Retail Project on June 1, Lisa had to rely on a "campaign summary" Word document that summarized the film, the issues raised by Wal-Mart, and the proposed action plan for Wal-Mart Week. Although Lisa was able to show a trailer to potential partners at in-person meetings, until June 1 she was not allowed to send out the trailer on DVD or post it on the web.

Lisa recommends that all filmmakers prepare a "campaign summary" document, even those who already have a website and press clippings about their film-in-progress. A written description of the campaign helps all of the parties rally around a concrete plan, and often stimulates debate and discussion that generates new ideas and techniques.

An introduction from a mutual friend or colleague is always helpful, but Lisa says that many important partnerships are built by a filmmaker cold-calling

the high cost of low price

relevant organizations. She recommends checking the organization's website to find the name of an executive director, outreach coordinator, or public relations manager who could be the initial point of contact. "Once the value of film as an organizing tool is understood, the plotting and planning can begin," Lisa reports. "Organizing screenings is the fun part. Groups can charge admission and sell DVDs to raise awareness and funds for their organization. Ideally, we're providing a means to educate, motivate, and activate their constituents, and everyone wins!"

Energizing the partner organizations is one of the four main reasons Robert is going public with the project six months before Wal-Mart Week. June 1 originally became a target date because of the June 3 annual Wal-Mart shareholders' meeting. Announcing the film just forty-eight hours before Wal-Mart's annual pep rally seemed like a powerful shot across the bow that might influence press coverage of the shareholders' meeting.

Another hope is that the initial burst of publicity could motivate a guilt-stricken Wal-Mart executive to defect from the dark side. According to Jim, several senior executives at Fox News Channel sent anonymous e-mails to Robert when *Outfoxed* came out, offering inside information and confirmation of the allegations Robert made in his film. This valuable information was most appreciated, but was of limited use because it arrived after the film was completed.

Robert's team has been investigating Wal-Mart for six months, and like a crime investigation, many potential sources are reluctant to talk, for fear of reprisal. Just as a police chief publicizes a case in the hope of causing previously unknown sources to come forward, the *New York Times* piece and subsequent publicity may create a break in Robert's case against Wal-Mart.

The final reason to go public at this early stage is the possibility of raising serious money from the public. The Dean campaign, MoveOn.org, and other activist organizations proved in the 2004 presidential election that an internet-connected group can raise big money by motivating a large number of people to make small donations on their credit cards. Whether or not the Retail Project can raise significant funds from the public depends on how much traffic can be driven to WalMartMovie.com.

On Tuesday, May 31, Robert boards a plane for Washington, DC. He will be attending the Take Back America conference on Wednesday when the news breaks. Robert also intends to speak to the fifty Democracy for America meetings Wednesday evening via a conference call from Washington.

Since the *New York Times* has demanded exclusivity on the story, Robert's official press release announcing the Wal-Mart movie cannot hit the wire services until 10:00 a.m. EST on Wednesday. Whether or not the *Times* article will generate additional media opportunities remains to be seen. It would be great if Robert could appear on radio and television on Wednesday or Thursday, setting the table for Wal-Mart's shareholders' meeting on Friday. Nobody knows if this is doable or not, but the answer will be revealed in the next few hours...

WAL★MART
the high cost of low price

Gone Public

The morning of June 1, Jim sits in front of his two computer screens, monitoring web traffic to his just-launched WalMartMovie.com. Traffic is light. Although the *New York Times* article is being read by thousands of people, the article did not include a link to WalMartMovie.com, so people have no idea where to go for more information on the film.

The problem is compounded by the fact that search engines like Google and Yahoo have not yet flagged WalMartMovie.com as a popular destination for web surfers. So when users search for "Wal-Mart Movie," they are not seeing Robert's new site at the top of the list, since the web is saturated with references to Wal-Mart and the thousands of movies they carry on DVD. (As a stopgap measure, Jim purchased Google advertisements for the keywords "Wal-Mart Movie," "Wal-Mart Documentary," and "Wal-Mart Greenwald," to make sure that a "sponsored link" to WalMartMovie.com appeared prominently on appropriate searches.)

But Jim has not yet deployed his big weapon: an outgoing

e-mail blast to nearly 70,000 of Robert's previous customers for *Outfoxed* and *Uncovered*. Between people who purchased these DVDs directly from Robert's company, and others who signed up to receive e-mail updates about these films, Robert's list contains some of the individuals most likely to get involved at this early stage.

Jim's e-mail blast goes out at 10:00 a.m. EST. The idea is to hit people while they are at their desks. Jim knows that recipients are more likely to open an e-mail that arrives while they are at work than one that arrives during off-hours or over the weekend.

Traffic at WalMartMovie.com immediately spikes, as recipients of Jim's mass e-mail begin visiting the website, signing up to host screenings and making donations on their credit cards. Jim can track many different variables: the time of day that e-mails are opened, the particular link that a user clicks on, how users navigate through WalMartMovie.com, etc. Jim e-mails Robert some early statistics on donations and web traffic. Robert is at the Take Back America conference, reading his e-mails on the Blackberry and responding when he can.

By 3:00 p.m., Jim is pretty pumped. Donations have been rolling in, totaling more than $10,000 in the first five hours since the e-mail blast. With the exception of a thousand-dollar donation, all the contributions are small amounts, between twenty and a hundred dollars.

Another encouraging sign is the reaction by the "blogosphere." Almost immediately after the *New York Times* story went up on the web, bloggers started republishing the story along with a link to WalMartMovie.com. Within forty-eight hours, there are more than fifty blogs that have mentioned Robert's movie, and almost every blog posting includes a link to WalMartMovie.com. Robert helped trigger this blogalanche with his own Wednesday morning missive that appeared on

the high cost of low price

the brand-new "Huffington Post" megablog run by Arianna Huffington. (In his "Huffington Post" blog entry, Robert accidentally referred to Medicaid as Medicare, a slip which was pointed out by several bloggers later in the day.)

Reviewing site traffic on Thursday, Jim can see that the blogs represent the second biggest source of incoming visitors to WalMartMovie.com, trailing only the visitors who got an e-mail from Jim's Wednesday morning blast. The range of blogs covering the story is impressive, including labor-oriented blogs, business-oriented blogs, urban planning and land use blogs, and blogs that are focused on Wal-Mart and other big-box retailers.

Producer Jim Gilliam monitors web traffic at his desk.

On Friday, the Wal-Mart shareholders' meeting takes place, and Robert's film is mentioned in several newspaper articles that list the various groups protesting Wal-Mart's business practices. In the wake of Wednesday's *New York Times* piece, the mainstream print media has been slow to publish their own feature stories about Robert's new film. Perhaps the business writers aren't used to covering a documentary film, and the arts writers aren't ready to deal with a film that won't be released until November.

Interest from television has been much higher. Some of the biggest television news shows have been calling Ken Sunshine, Robert's publicist in New York. Bookers for these shows want to know one thing: What does Robert have on Wal-Mart, and is he ready to reveal it?

He's not. Robert wants to hold back specifics on the film until later in the campaign, to make sure Wal-Mart is not given a head-start in planning their public rebuttal of the film. The bookers have given Robert a powerful message: In order to put Robert on network television, he's going to have to deliver something juicy. During a staff meeting the next Monday, Robert reminds his co-producers that the film will need to include some real scoops, previously untold stories that reveal new information about Wal-Mart and its business practices. Although no footage has been shot as of yet, the crime story seems like one of the issues most likely to create a media sensation come November.

Also on Monday, Jim Gilliam compiles all of the launch data into a report for the Tuesday staff meeting. Incoming contributions now total $26,117 from 655 donors. The pace of donations has been slowing down. So has traffic to WalMart-Movie.com. Jim is convinced that outgoing e-mails are the key to further spreading the word. Activating the partner organizations to e-mail their members about the Retail Project is going to be a major priority in the days ahead.

Robert is encouraged by Jim's progress report, but he's starting to have second thoughts about the title of the film. The agent of doubt is Berkeley linguistics professor George Lakoff, whose book *Don't Think Like an Elephant: Know Your Values and Frame the Debate* became required reading for progressives in 2004. Lakoff is one of Robert's many informal advisors, and Robert asked him for feedback on the movie title when they saw each other in Washington, DC last week at the Take Back America conference.

In his book, Lakoff suggests that American conservatives use strategically-chosen language in their communications

the high cost of low price

about political issues. The language is often chosen to "reframe" an issue, attaching new connotations that have a subtle yet powerful effect on public perception. One of Lakoff's examples is the way that Republicans relabeled the "Estate Tax" as the "Death Tax." Whereas most Americans can't relate to having an "Estate," they certainly can relate to the inevitability of death. The "Estate Tax" sounds like something that affects only those people who have estates, while the "Death Tax" sounds like an unfair burden on everyone who dies. (The IRS website says that the Estate Tax only affects the wealthiest two percent of Americans, those who leave more than a million dollars to their heirs.)

The first page of Lakoff's book issues a warning to political communicators: "When you are arguing against the other side: Do not use their language. Their language picks out a frame—and it won't be the frame you want." In his conversation with Robert, Lakoff raised the following question: "What if the reference to low prices reinforces Wal-Mart's own frame? If the low prices are the thing that people most like about Wal-Mart, why include that favorable characteristic in the title of your movie?"

Thinking about Lakoff's comments, Robert remembered an earlier occasion where the quality of a name was in question. In early 2005, Robert was looking for a name for his new documentary company, and decided to seek ideas from the readers of his blog. Robert offered a box set of his documentaries to whoever suggested the name that Robert chose for his new company. Hundreds of names were submitted, many of them quite good. Robert and his team ended up selecting the submission "Brave New Films," and they've been quite happy with both the name and the naming process.

So Robert decides to seek a little feedback from the public on "The High Cost of Low Price." At 4:30 p.m. on June 13, Robert posts a simple note on his blog asking readers for their thoughts on the existing title, and for ideas on alternatives. The next morning, Jim e-mails Robert's "Name That Film!" challenge to the several thousand people who have already signed up to receive WalMartMovie.com news updates.

The response is instant and cacophonous. By noon, there are already 100 comments posted on Robert's blog, many of which contain multiple suggestions. This flood of incoming communications makes Robert almost giddy with delight. "I didn't really get the internet until someone told me it was a conversation, rather than a monologue," he explains. Beyond the value of market-testing the movie title, the exercise has shown Robert how passionate his audience is about the movie, which is a great shot in the arm.

Robert and Jim have also been monitoring reaction from another important component of the film's audience: Wal-Mart itself. During the spring, Jim had often wondered how Wal-Mart would react to the first news about the film. Would they take the bait, denouncing the film and fueling a public relations fire? Or would Wal-Mart follow the traditional corporate media strategy and keep their comments to a minimum?

In the first two weeks of June, Wal-Mart's reaction to the film has been limited to a pair of comments the company provided for the June 1 *Times* story. When first asked for a comment by the *Times* reporter, Wal-Mart's spokesperson provided the company's standard quote about the "narrow self-interest" of Wal-Mart's critics. The same quote used in the *Times* article appeared in at least two other articles that week. In three different publications, Wal-Mart spokespeople referred to different critics of the company using almost exactly the same words.

"Some of our critics are open-minded people who are genuinely concerned about issues and want to make the world a better place," Wal-Mart spokesperson Sarah Clark told the *Times*. "We listen, learn, and try to work with them toward

the high cost of low price

common goals. Other groups simply pull publicity stunts to further their own narrow self-interest."

At the top of Wal-Mart's "self-interested" list are the UFCW's "Wake-Up Wal-Mart" and the SEIU's "Wal-Mart Watch." Each organization's logo is prominently featured on the "Host a Screening" page at WalMartMovie.com. In her dealings with Wake-Up Wal-Mart in May, Lisa inadvertently triggered a leak that was exploited by Wal-Mart as the *Times* article neared publication.

After Lisa made a "let's get excited" presentation to the UFCW via a conference call, someone on the call posted an item about Robert's upcoming movie on the "American Street" blog. The post appeared in the last week of May, and it seems that Wal-Mart immediately detected the post. As the *Times* writer was completing his story, Sarah Clark contacted him again to highlight the connection between the movie and the UFCW.

"We'd question the fairness of a documentary that is being tied to the Wake-Up Wal-Mart Campaign," Clark told the *Times*. "And I'd certainly question the accuracy or the fairness of a documentary that didn't even contact us," she continued.

Robert's staffers who lived through the *Outfoxed* media battle with News Corp are scrutinizing Wal-Mart's comments for any clues about the company's PR strategy. Are Clark's quotes a sign that Wal-Mart intends to portray Robert as a tool of the labor movement? And did Clark crack the door open for Robert to ask a senior Wal-Mart exec to be interviewed on camera?

WAL★MART
the high cost of low price

Comedy
Spots

Within the first forty-eight hours of the launch of WalMartMovie.com, hundreds of people volunteered via e-mail to help Robert finish the movie. One of those volunteers was actress Frances Fisher, who is best known for playing Kate Winslet's mother in "Titanic." Frances found out about the Retail Project from a politically-active friend the day after the *Times* story was published. After browsing around the WalMartMovie.com website, Frances linked into RobertGreenwald.org and e-mailed Robert a note. She said she was passionate about the issues raised in Robert's new movie and offered to help out in any way that she could.

Frances expected to receive an automated response or a form letter. Instead, she got a personal e-mail from Robert within the hour. He told Frances that he might have a role for her, and to expect to hear from one of his producers very soon. Robert remembered working with Frances on "The Audrey Hepburn Story," a made-for-TV movie that he produced in 2000.

Thirty minutes later, Frances got a second e-mail, this time from Laurie Levit, who asked Frances if she could appear in a Wal-Mart parody ad that would be shot on Wednesday, June 7 in Santa Monica.

A former television producer, Laurie abruptly quit show business twelve years ago while producing a made-for-TV movie in Vancouver. One night she was going over the shooting script with a middle-aged B-list actor. Laurie's daughter burst in the hotel room, upset about having a bad dream. The actor shot Laurie a look that said "it's the kid or me," and as soon as the project was completed, Laurie chose the kid. Permanently. Or so she thought.

Laurie had recently told Robert she was feeling a bit bored as a full-time mom. Robert suggested she come to one of his Tuesday afternoon staff meetings, and within the week she was on board to produce a dozen "comedy spots" for the Retail Project.

Robert envisioned these comedy spots as comic relief for an otherwise earnest and somber film. Inspired by the propagandistic Americana of Wal-Mart's own advertising, Robert wanted to create sarcastic parody ads like the ones featured on "Saturday Night Live," and use these spots as interstitials between the various segments of his documentary. The spots could also be made available on WalMartMovie.com in the fall to build excitement about Wal-Mart Week.

Since most of Robert's career has been in the world of scripted movies, he figured there were plenty of writers, actors, and crew people he could call upon to help him create these parody ads. Many of Robert's associates in the film and TV business are politically active on left-of-center causes and often work together on political projects. But he had no idea what he would run up against in soliciting Hollywood for help on a film critical of Wal-Mart.

Wal-Mart is the nation's biggest seller of movies on DVD.

the high cost of low price

Movie stars, studio heads, and other industry luminaries regularly make special trips to Bentonville to get Wal-Mart's management fired up about promoting particular movies. Obtaining prime positioning on Wal-Mart's shelves and end-caps is key to a major motion picture's success on DVD.

When Laurie Levit started calling friends and colleagues looking for help on the Wal-Mart parody spots, she ran into a brick wall. "The fear is all-pervasive," she said. "Actors are afraid to appear in the spots. Writers and producers worry about Wal-Mart refusing to carry their future productions. Even the twenty-somethings on my crew are afraid to appear on camera as extras."

That's why Frances Fisher's e-mail of Thursday, June 2 was so useful. Laurie had been trying to cast the role of "Wendy" for weeks now, to play opposite the well-known character actor James Cromwell. Famous for his role as Farmer Hoggett in *Babe*, Cromwell is a longtime activist on environmental, animal rights, and nuclear power issues.

When approached by his agent with a chance to spend a morning working for union scale on an anti-Wal-Mart spot, Cromwell jumped at the opportunity. "Any chance to piss on Wal-Mart, and I'm in," he exclaimed.

Cromwell, who goes by the nickname Jamie, was cast as "Bob," a small-town retiree who loves to sit on the porch with his wife "Wendy." Having landed such a well-known actor for Bob, Laurie was desperate to cast an equally distinguished actor as his wife.

Laurie pounced on the chance to cast Frances Fisher as Wendy, but there was one hitch. Frances didn't live in Los Angeles. Frances resides in Carmel, California, six hours north. She was happy to be asked, but wasn't sure that child-care and travel arrangements could be worked out on such short notice.

Laurie continued trying to cast the role of Wendy over

the weekend. Once she found out Frances lived upstate, getting her onboard seemed like a longshot, especially since Laurie did not have any money in the budget for travel expenses. But on Monday morning, Laurie got a new e-mail from Frances, pleading "don't give away my part!"

Later that day, Frances found a friend who would be flying down to Los Angeles by private jet on Wednesday morning. All Frances needed from the Retail Project was a rental car and a coach-class ticket to return home on Wednesday afternoon. "Done!" exclaimed Laurie, and Frances was officially "in."

* * *

At 9:00 a.m. on Wednesday, June 7, Frances and Jamie are safely ensconced on an old-fashioned porch, looking like they've been sitting there for decades. The porch is at the front of a beautifully-restored craftsman house on one of the toniest streets in Santa Monica. Wrapped in blossoming rosebushes, the porch could be located in Anytown, USA.

A crew of eleven has been setting up for two hours, placing baffles around the porch to control the direct sunlight. Three modestly-sized lights on tall stands look down on Bob and Wendy from above. With all the gear surrounding them, Bob

Actors James Cromwell and Frances Fisher as "Bob and Wendy."

and Wendy cannot be seen except from the camera's position.

The camera being used today is the same Panasonic DVX-100a used by the co-producers. But today the little Panasonic is heavily accessorized with narrative filmmaking's "tools of the trade." There's a filter box attached to the lens, and a gear-driven manual focus control at the cameraman's left hand. The camera is attached to a standard tripod via a mini-jib, a counterweighted eight-foot arm that can be moved smoothly in any direction with just a fingertip.

The jib is necessary because the director is trying to reproduce the look of Wal-Mart's own homespun advertising. Wal-Mart's ads use soft focus and warm lighting to convey the romance of small-town USA, with a gently-moving camera that connotes authenticity and informality. The little jib will give the director the ability to move the camera up, down, right, and left just like the fancy camera-moves in Wal-Mart's own ads.

The director is listed on the call sheet as "Alan Smithee," Hollywood's code for "unwilling to be named." He's an experienced television director specializing in multi-camera sitcoms. With the sitcom becoming an endangered species, he's working hard to transition to the single-camera world of television drama and feature film. Although he does have a sitcom gig lined up for the fall, he's eager to get some single-camera experience and happy to direct Laurie's spots. As long as nobody knows he's here.

The crew is comprised of young people building up their credits and experience. There's an assistant director, a sound person, a few gaffers wrangling the small compliment of lights and stands, and a video playback operator. The one Retail Project "regular" is Kristy's husband Chris Bottoms, who handles her cinematographer duties whenever she's out of town.

So far everything's going smoothly. The objective was to be rolling tape by 9:00 a.m., completing four "Bob and Wendy" spots by 1:00, when Jamie needs to leave for the set of "Six Feet Under." Jamie and Frances are taking their jobs seriously, quietly rehearsing their lines, discussing the characters' attitudes and motivations, and working through the timing of the punch lines with the director.

The "Bob and Wendy" spots are a playful yet dark look at what happens when Wal-Mart comes to town. Written by a posse of Emmy-winning screenwriters who are friends of Laurie's, the spots reveal Bob and Wendy to be cheerful, up-with-progress fans of Wal-Mart even as the superstore's arrival creates traffic headaches, environmental pollution, and a boarded-up-downtown.

When the actors are ready to attempt their first take, the director yells "action!" Holding glasses of lemonade, Jamie and Frances talk about the new Wal-Mart that's just opened. "No need to go all the way downtown anymore," chirps Frances. After completing her final line, Frances looks at Jamie, they clink glasses, and she sips, gurgles, chokes, and coughs.

Everybody laughs. "That lemonade is strong stuff!" she shouts, recovering her composure. The first take was spot-on until the lemonade hit Frances' lips.

The actors reset, and run another take. "Perfect!" exclaims the director. "I don't hear that word very often," says Frances coyly. "I don't say it very often," replies the flattering director. It's a rare moment of apple-polishing during the making of Robert's documentary, where the prevailing tone is friendly sarcasm.

The director supervises additional takes for "coverage" purposes. He shoots the thirty-second spot as a master shot, as a two-shot, and as a close-up on each of the two actors. The various angles can be cut together in a variety of ways, giving the editors lots of choices. The director does one final take where the camera floats into the porch after passing under a tree branch. Watching the monitor, soft-focus leaves in the foreground give way to Bob and Wendy on the porch, with the same idealized tone as Wal-Mart's own spots.

Laurie worked her connections to get access to this fancy soundstage for the day. As a thank-you gesture to her friend who booked the soundstage, Laurie cast the woman's hus-

the high cost of low price

band as a Wal-Mart manager in one of the spots.

All of today's spots take place inside of a Wal-Mart store. Since filming the actors in an actual Wal-Mart wasn't possible, Laurie and the director were faced with three choices: film in a discount store similar to a Wal-Mart, create a set that looked like a Wal-Mart, or shoot the actors against a green screen and then superimpose them on video footage of a Wal-Mart interior.

Laurie and the director preferred the green screen approach, provided that good background footage could be obtained. Then somebody realized that the Retail Project already had a huge library of Wal-Mart interior footage, courtesy of the "Opening Days" project.

The assistant editors compiled a reel of the best Wal-Mart interior footage shot by the amateur and semi-pro videographers Sarah hired back in January to film the grand opening of fifty new Wal-Mart stores. The quality of the footage was surprisingly good, and Laurie and the director decided to move forward with the green screen approach for today's comedy spots.

This morning, the director and Laurie talked through the creative direction for today's shoot. Should the crew be aiming for maximum realism, trying to make it look like the actors really are inside a Wal-Mart? Or should the goal be a campy, goofy approach where the green-screen technique is obvious and makes the whole viewing experience that much more funny?

Together they decide that the crew will start off trying for maximum realism. If the results are good, they'll stick with that approach. If the green screen effect has a natural cheesiness to it, then they'll embrace the cheese and go campy.

Within an hour it becomes clear that a startling degree of realism can be obtained. This particular soundstage has been optimized for green screen shooting. The green vertical wall curves gently as it approaches the floor, ensuring that no corner can be seen by the camera. The wall is lit by a permanent lighting system hanging from a pipe grid. Controlled by a dimmer board, the lights have been calibrated to create a perfectly uniform brightness across the entire green wall.

An actor wearing an eBay-obtained Wal-Mart vest stands about ten feet in front of the green wall. She's playing a Wal-Mart associate who cheerfully greets her co-workers and then whispers to the camera, "I don't even know that person. Is she new?"

Actor plays a Wal-Mart associate in front of the green screen.

Although the camera itself is shooting the actor against the green background, the crew has set up a monitor that simulates how the actor will look when she is superimposed on the Wal-Mart interior footage. The assistant director has dozens of video clips on his Mac laptop, instantly accessible in a Final Cut Pro timeline. At the beginning of each setup, the director selects a "plate" from the variety of Wal-Mart interior shots. The "plate" chosen for this particular shot is a long Wal-Mart aisle receding back into the distance.

Studying the monitor, Chris calls for subtle adjustments to the lights that are pointed at the actor, trying to match the light sources in the "plate." Since this plate is a store aisle lit from above by fluorescent tubes, Chris is lighting the actor on our soundstage so that she appears to be lit from above by fluorescent tubes.

the high cost of low price

Beyond matching the lighting, matching the scale between actor and plate is also important. If the camera zooms too close to the actor, the actor will appear too tall for the Wal-Mart aisle, and if the camera pulls back too much, the actor will appear too short.

It's a trial and error process involving a lot of careful fine-tuning. Yet rather than being tedious, it feels delightful. Even though everyone on the crew has worked on green screen shoots before, the superimposition of a moving person on top of video that shows other moving persons is a naturally funny thing. Every few minutes there's a "gee whiz" moment when the foreground and background match up perfectly. It's even funnier because the crew can see the actor in her Wal-Mart employee vest standing in front of a bright green wall, and at the same time can look at the little monitor and see her standing in front of a busy Wal-Mart aisle in which shoppers pass behind her with their carts.

The next day, Robert reviews footage from the green-screen shoot with Laurie and Jim. Jim is giggling. He can't believe how the footage looks completely real. Robert is smiling quietly. At the end of the playback, he pauses and then muses aloud, "Hmmm...you could make an entire movie as if it took place inside a Wal-Mart."

WAL★MART
the high cost of low price

Outside Counsel

A week after Robert issued his "Name the Film!" challenge, there are over 450 comments posted on his blog, and over a thousand potential movie titles to choose from. Jim finds the whole thing too delightful to kill off. "By opening it up for suggestions, Robert is giving people a feeling of ownership about his film. We're gathering new e-mail addresses, people are signing up to host screenings—we just *have* to keep it going."

In Jim's mind, the next step is obvious. Cull the best suggestions, and put it to a vote. Whatever title is the most popular becomes the new name of the film. Let the people's voice be heard!

Robert isn't so sure about this plan. Getting suggestions from the public is one thing, but giving up the power to choose the title of his own movie is quite another. Yet Jim keeps pushing, taking an informal poll of the staff to whittle down the initial list. The kitschy "Wal-Mart: The Movie!" is an in-house favorite, and becomes one of four finalists. Jim takes another step forward, preparing a special webpage where the public could vote. Now all that remains is getting Robert's blessing to move forward.

Taking a break from building the voting page, Jim writes a post for his own blog, JimGilliam.com. Jim posts once or twice a week, providing insider tidbits to the hardcore of Robert's fan base. Jim's post for today is about a book he's reading with the provocative title *All Marketers Are Liars*. Jim posts a brief but flavorful excerpt from the book, which is written by Seth Godin, one of the many marketing geniuses spawned by the dotcom revolution.

Godin's previous book, *Permission Marketing*, extolled the benefits of establishing a relationship with potential customers by inviting them to sign up to receive occasional e-mails. His premise is that a consumer who invites you to communicate with her is a far better sales prospect than someone who receives unwelcome junk mail.

Permission marketing is a key part of Jim's own strategy for the Retail Project, but it still comes as a surprise when a personal e-mail from Seth Godin appears in Jim's inbox less than twenty-four hours after Jim blogged about Godin's book. Sent on June 19, Godin's e-mail is brief but intriguing: "The work you do is so important...if I can help, I'd like to try. – Seth"

Jim immediately e-mails back, saying "Thank you! That means a lot. Would love to get you involved, but can't imagine we can afford you."

Jim assumes that Seth discovered Jim's blog post by using the blog search engine Technorati.com. "I guess if he's clever at marketing other people's products, he uses the same techniques in marketing himself and his books," Jim says. "He must monitor net chatter about his books pretty closely."

Within a few hours, Jim receives a second e-mail from Seth that contains just five words: "I'm free. As in zero." Jim jumps at the opportunity to get some no-fee advice, and arranges for Seth to call in to the next Brave New Films marketing meeting.

the high cost of low price

Filmmaker's Toolbox:
Building and Managing an E-mail List

Permission marketing has fueled the emergence of a new generation of political groups across the ideological spectrum. Twenty years ago, advocacy organizations used direct mail as their primary means of attracting and retaining members. The high cost of designing, printing, stuffing, and sending thousands of solicitations and newsletters limited the growth of smaller groups and kept the long-established, well-funded organizations at the forefront.

Internet communication has caused a paradigm shift in the world of nonprofits and advocacy groups, making it possible for millions of people to rapidly coalesce around emerging issues using websites and e-newsletters. While direct mail is still a powerful tool for organizations that can afford it, the new generation of wired organizations uses e-mail as their primary tool to communicate with members and raise funds.

Yet building and managing an e-mail list can rapidly outgrow the capabilities of Microsoft Outlook and a personal e-mail account. Just as large companies spend an increasing amount of money on software for "customer relationship management," nonprofits and advocacy groups are deploying an ever-growing arsenal of web-based tools to create sophisticated interactive communities.

Howard Dean's presidential campaign popularized

many of these new technologies and techniques in 2003, as internet fund-raising helped Dean move from dark horse to front-runner in the months leading up to the Iowa Caucus. Other candidates quickly deployed Dean's innovations, building the foundation for a new e-services industry catering to the needs of nonprofits and political advocacy groups.

For the Retail Project, Jim Gilliam selected a service provider called Democracy In Action, a Washington, DC company founded in 2003. With a powerful database to store subscriber information and an easy-to-use point-and-click interface, the Democracy In Action service frees Jim from the tedious process of building these capabilities from scratch. From tracking click-through rates to processing credit-card donations, the Democracy In Action platform automates many of the activities that have become the building blocks of today's e-activism.

Several other companies are creating new services based on an open-source technology platform developed by CivicSpace Labs. As of this writing, the website of one of these firms, Echoditto.com, contains a "Best Practices" section with a variety of useful information, including how to write the most effective fundraising e-mails. Since the world of nonprofits and advocacy groups is based on networking and information-sharing, there are several very useful blogs that discuss e-strategies and evaluate the latest innovations in electronic-based advocacy.

On the morning of June 23, Jim, Lisa, Devin, and Rick are huddled around the phone in Robert's office. Robert is calling in from home. At exactly 10:30 a.m., marketing genius Seth Godin joins the conference call, and Robert thanks him for taking the time to brainstorm.

Seth asks Robert's team to fill him in on the grass-roots techniques they plan to use in marketing the Wal-Mart film. Jim gives a brief description of the key points, including the house parties, the WalMartMovie.com site, and the high-profile launch of Wal-Mart Week in November.

In Yoda-esque fashion, Seth pauses and then delivers simple yet meaningful advice.

"Right now, the number of people willing to embrace the film is a small, already-converted group. The website is preaching to the already-activated, and giving them something exciting to do. That is the right place to be at this early stage.

"There's a much bigger group you want to reach who are not comfortable joining up at this point. Down the road, you need to find a way to get to people who need to see validation of the movie by reading a review or hearing about it from a friend. How can you get the film to move from hand to hand, so people who may not want to participate in a demonstration will have a low-risk way to spread the word?"

Jim, Rick, and Lisa look at each other and nod in silent approval as Seth continues. "The question is how to instantly activate the people attending the first week of screenings so that you exponentially grow the audience. At the end of the film, people will be motivated at that very moment. You gotta have something actionable for them to do right away."

Then Seth serves up the Big Idea. What if house party organizers make the following offer to attendees: "Give me fifty dollars and I'll give you ten DVDs packed in ready-to-mail sleeves for you to send to your friends." Jim does a back-of-the-napkin calculation out loud. "If we meet our goal of 7,000 house parties, that's maybe 200,000 attendees. If half of the attendees send out a ten-pack of DVDs, that's one million DVDs!"

According to Seth, the million DVDs are likely to be put to good use. "There are very few people who will not start watching a DVD that has arrived from someone they know," he explains. "The perceived value of a feature film on DVD is twenty dollars, and that makes people want to watch it."

Everybody is captivated with the idea of "exponentially" expanding the audience in the days that follow Wal-Mart Week. Seth agrees to make himself available for future consultation, and signs off. Robert stays on, expressing his enthusiasm. "This was great. There are people who know this shit better than we do, and we need to keep bringing them in." Robert turns his attention to practicalities. "What are the logistics of doing it, and how can we raise the money to fund it?"

It's agreed that Jim will draft an action plan for the Million-DVD idea, so that Rick can start pitching it to donors in an effort to raise the money necessary to make it happen. Jim is surprised at his own passion for Seth's advice. "Even I, the guy who has been running around and saying all this stuff about interactivity, feel excited hearing it said so clearly and simply," he gushes. Chalk up another victory for the informal network of the blogosphere.

WAL★MART
the high cost of low price

Upstairs, Downstairs, and Overseas

Inspired by one of Robert's new ideas, editor Doug Cheek has made what appears to be a breakthrough. In the course of a week, he's put together a twenty-minute assembly of soundbites that radically alters the film's rhythm. Usually hunched over his computer wearing headphones and scowling at the monitors, Doug's mood is buoyant today, as he shows his new work to Kerry during a lunch break.

The tempo and texture of Doug's new section feels nothing like the existing segments. Rather than staying in one town with a single group of characters, Doug's new section jumps around, smashing together related comments from people all over the country. New characters appear without introduction, and often the viewer has no idea of their names or where they live. The one thing they have in common is that they are former Wal-Mart associates.

Robert's been talking a lot about structure in the past few weeks. Confident that the co-producers have obtained good material on most of the key topics, Robert has turned his attention to the question of how to best organize all of this material. His various script outlines over the last six months have been organized as a linear progression of social and political issues. Ten days ago, he had an idea about dividing the film into two sections: "People" and "Places." "People" would explore Wal-Mart's impact on its own employees, and "Places" would pursue Wal-Mart's impact on cities and towns.

Doug's been assigned with taking a first crack at the "People" section. He's grouped together soundbites by topic, each introduced by a title card. The topics include "Making Ends Meet," "Seeking Public Assistance," "Gender Discrimination," and "Working Off-the-Clock." Each topic is explored by multiple interviewees sharing their personal stories of working at Wal-Mart. As Doug jump-cuts from person to person and state to state, the viewer is immersed in a three-dimensional experience of Wal-Mart's internal world. Rather than Robert's original concept of following a single Wal-Mart family, Doug has created a composite, kaleidoscopic portrait of life as a Wal-Mart associate.

Occasional comments by a trio of former Wal-Mart store managers add a sinister overlay to the "People" section. After a few associates tell their individual stories about a particular problem, Doug cuts to one of three former store managers for a look at the same issue through the eye of the Boss Man. Robert calls this format "Upstairs/Downstairs," a term made popular by the famous Masterpiece Theatre television melodrama of the same name. (The BBC's period piece explored the inner life of a British mansion, with maids and cooks toiling in the basement while their masters enjoyed fine food and wine in the upstairs parlor.)

"One of the purest and most wonderful things about film is putting two different images next to each other, and then one plus one equals three," says Robert. Late one night

the high cost of low price

at home, Robert was watching the store manager footage and realized that it would be most powerful if placed inside personal stories from the hourly associates.

In applying Robert's "Upstairs/Downstairs" concept, Doug has made Wheldon Nicholson a star, presenting the former store manager as the Dark Lord of Discounting. Describing Wal-Mart's employment practices, Wheldon channels the cold, steely store manager "doing what he has to do to get that next promotion." His tone of voice has an edge and a meanness that contrasts perfectly with the earnestness and sincerity of the hourly associates.

Robert working with editor Doug Cheek.

"Wheldon has turned out to be huge," exclaims Robert. "He spoke from the heart because this was the first time he was ever interviewed." In today's media-saturated environment, investigating a hot topic inevitably means running across interviewees who've told their story many times. The interviewee who can deliver new information in a fresh and unrehearsed manner is worth his weight in gold.

Another strength of Doug's segment is that every speaker is someone who worked at Wal-Mart. There's not a single outsider or "expert" in the whole twenty minutes. Robert's insistence that the co-producers shoot people while they are "doing something" pays off handsomely in this context, providing the viewer with an ever-shifting backdrop of living rooms, kitchen tables, backyards, and pickup trucks. The segment reads like a crazy quilt of everyday life, as the interviewees wash their cars and help the kids with homework. This richness of detail would be lost if each associate had sat for a carefully-lit, "60 Minutes" style interview.

Kerry's impressed with Doug's progress. As the editors finish their sandwiches, they ask Kerry to tell them a story about his China trip. Over the past two weeks, Kerry's brief, intense e-mails from the Shenzhen factory district have had the entire crew on pins and needles awaiting his safe return. "I'm going to tell you about the night when private security forces busted down the door of our hotel room," Kerry says in a soft voice, and the editors lean in to listen.

Several months in the making, Kerry's China trip was a mission to interview low-wage factory workers who make items that are sold in America at Wal-Mart. From the beginning, Robert and Kerry agreed that they would need a highly experienced guide to penetrate the murky world of Chinese manufacturing.

After interviewing several different filmmakers and journalists, Robert and Kerry decided to work with an operative code-named Cheetah, who had spent time in China making a documentary about workers in a jeans factory. Born in Taiwan, Cheetah has a keen understanding of globalization, speaks fluent Chinese and has practical experience blending in with Chinese workers; on her previous project Cheetah even convinced a factory owner to permit her to live in a workers' dormitory.

A tall Canadian with a shaggy Richard Gere haircut, Kerry knew he would stand out like a sore thumb in the factory towns of Shenzhen Province. So it would be up to Cheetah to make the contacts and do the filming. Kerry's role was akin to that of a CIA case officer, supervising the operation without

the high cost of low price

interjecting himself in the action. Cheetah has proven to be a gutsy and resourceful spy, infiltrating a factory by wearing a borrowed uniform and then filming the working conditions with a tiny camera in a small cardboard box tucked in her underarm.

Kerry begins his story. "So we're two-thirds into the trip, and I'm on the phone with Cheetah late at night. She's in a dingy hotel near the factories, and I'm in the business hotel used by westerners. Cheetah is telling me about the day's footage, and then, in mid-sentence, I hear a crash and men yelling. A half-dozen local policemen and private security guards have busted down the door of Cheetah's hotel room! I don't understand Chinese, but somehow the basic narrative is obvious. The security guards are yelling at Cheetah, demanding to know what she's doing in town. Where are her papers? Who has authorized her to be here? Cheetah, she's fearless, she's yelling right back at them. Finally, after ten minutes of screaming, the men leave and Cheetah fills me in on what happened."

Cheetah reacted to the intruders by waving around the business card of one of Shenzhen's many bureaucrats, whom she had dined with on a previous evening. "You want to fuck with me? Then I'll fuck with you and you won't have a job tomorrow morning," she fumed. The cops, poorly paid and low on the totem pole themselves, begged for mercy and retreated when faced with the prospect of getting in trouble with a government official.

Kerry continues his tale, explaining how he and Cheetah changed hotels later that evening as a safety precaution. Although her cover had been blown, Cheetah insisted on staying in town and finishing her remaining interviews with the workers. She saw several of the same cops on the street over the next few days, and none of them gave her any trouble at all.

The editors are enjoying Kerry's story, but none of them are eager to edit Kerry's footage. Cutting foreign-language material is one of the most time-consuming jobs in the edit bay. Doug, Chris, and Jonathan are hoping that the China segment is assigned to Robert Florio, "the night guy," who has come onboard this week to work opposite the three-man daytime team. Adding a night shift is a cost-saving measure, enabling Doug and Florio to share one edit system rather than incurring the cost of renting a fourth system.

Filmmaker's Toolbox: Licensing vs. Shooting Original Footage

The China footage is a good example of how a single line of inquiry can result in a big pile of bills. From research to travel to translation to editing, Robert's China effort will cost well into the five-figures. Could the Retail Project have made the connection between low-cost merchandise and low-wage labor by using licensed footage from one of the many existing documentaries about working conditions in Asia?

With hundreds of cable and satellite channels to feed, a growing number of producers are generating footage on virtually any topic imaginable, and much of this footage is available for a fee. Sources range from the established television networks and commercial video libraries all the way down to individual documentarians with unfinished projects. For example, when Robert was looking for material about a store Wal-Mart built at the foot of Mexico's most historic pyramid, he found a self-funded filmmaker from Puerto Rico who had

---

the high cost of low price

covered this particular site fight for an as-yet-unedited documentary film. (The Retail Project ended up using news clips to tell the story.)

Licensing existing footage always involves financial and creative tradeoffs. The more established sources charge a hefty fee for each second of footage, and the footage can sometimes appear generic or vaguely familiar. Individual documentarians often have fresher, more unique material, but are generally fearful of licensing any footage until after their own documentary is completed and released.

For the China story, Robert's been pushing the investigative team for something sharper, better, and more unique than what's available off-the-shelf, and he's been willing to back up his demands with his wallet. "China was not necessary to the story from a strictly narrative point of view," Robert explains. "After all, it moves us to another country late in the film. But I felt it was important to personalize the China story and help demystify and make human the Chinese workers. In the process it would become implicitly clear, without lecturing, that the enemy is not the Chinese people, but rather the policies of large corporations."

Before an editor can start work on the China segment, Kerry's many hours of footage need to be transcribed and translated. Even Cheetah herself doesn't understand some of the interviewees who use a regional dialect. During yesterday's crew meeting, Robert was pushing for all the China tapes to be translated in the next seven days. Sarah raised her hand with a point of information: "It can take six or even eight hours to translate a one-hour interview. We would probably need three full-time translators to get all the China tapes done in a week."

😊 What's in a Name?

On June 19, Robert agreed to let the public pick the title of his Wal-Mart documentary. "I was having a tough time getting Robert to give up the control at first," Jim explains. "But a few days later he suddenly decided he'd spent far too much time on this issue, and chose to leave it to me to sort it out." Robert subsequently approved Jim's list of finalists, and on June 22, the polls were opened.

Jim's June 23 e-mail to the WalMartMovie.com subscribers offered voters the choice of three titles and four subtitles:

For Title:
"Wal-Mart" (suggested by Sam Walton)
"Wal-Marked" (suggested by Jim Crawford)
"Wal-Marted" (suggested by Barbara Shadden Crow and Anonymous)

For Subtitle:
"Consuming America" (suggested by Cordell)

"Discounting America" (suggested by Jen Pfaff)
"The High Cost of Low Price" (the current subtitle)
"The Movie" (suggested by C. Cramer, John L., Eric Jaffa, and Woody Hastings)

Two days after the opening of the polls, the staff's favorite title, "Wal-Mart: The Movie," is taking a beating with the public, having received less than five percent of the votes. Voting will be open for five more days, with Robert announcing the winning title on June 29 during a live chat on his blog. According to Jim, these early returns are an important reality check, indicating that what feels kitschy-cool in Hollywood might not play in Peoria.

Jim is eager to apply this informal market research process to another element of the campaign: the official movie poster. Over the last few days, Robert has been working with an illustrator to finalize the poster art so that it can be digitally unveiled during the live chat that will announce the winning movie title.

For the poster, Robert's illustrator has created a suburban streetscape that's being devoured by a suit-wearing giant with six arms. The giant is in the process of scooping up people and cars, laying waste to homes and driveways in the process. The giant's head is a big yellow disc that looks almost like the Wal-Mart smiley-face.

Depicted with heavy, furrowed brows, and a huge hill-shaped frown, the yellow-headed marauding businessmonster looks mean and angry. Jim feels that the monster representing Wal-Mart should be enjoying himself as he rampages through small towns. And why alter the original smiley-face, an internationally-recognized classic?

Wal-Mart uses the black-on-yellow smiley-face in advertising and in their stores, even hiring actors to appear at Wal-Mart store openings wearing a giant yellow smiley head.

the high cost of low price

Sometimes Wal-Mart refers to the smiley figure as Rollback Man, because he smiles as he rolls back prices for the consumer. Although Wal-Mart neither invented nor owns the smiley-face design, many Americans now identify the smiley as a Wal-Mart branded character.

Jim's Evil Smiley and the original frowning smiley.

The original yellow smiley-face was in fact created for an insurance company back in 1963 by Harvey R. Ball. A graphic designer in Worcester, Massachusetts, Ball was paid forty-five dollars for his efforts. Ball never copyrighted his smiley-face design, which features two eyes, and a broad u-shaped smile. A decade later, Ball made no royalties from the smiley-face craze of 1972, when an estimated 50 million smiley-face buttons and mugs were sold in the United States. Sometime after the smiley-craze died down, Wal-Mart began using the design.

On June 28, Robert e-mails Jim the completed movie poster, ready to be shared with the participants in tomorrow's live chat. Once again, Jim suggests that the six-armed monster should be smiling, not frowning, and once more Robert rebuffs him.

Jim's already been using his own special version of the

smiley-face on WalMartMovie.com, prominently placed front-and-center at the top of the page. Jim refers to his version of the smiley-face as "Evil Smiley." While the classic smiley-face has no eyebrows, Evil Smiley has straight-line eyebrows that form a "V" between his eyes, adding a menacing intensity to his grin.

Filmmaker's Toolbox:
Spurring E-Subscribers to Action

Today's e-activists are constantly experimenting with new ways to communicate with their members. Because people use the internet differently than the way they read the newspaper or watch television, wired organizations study their members' click-through patterns, searching for information on how best to take advantage of this new medium. As e-activism matures, organizations are keeping a close eye on several key themes, including:

Frequency: How often should an organization e-mail its subscribers? If communication is too rare, you never build a community of shared interests. Yet if you pester your subscribers too often, you can turn them off, triggering a click on the dreaded "unsubscribe" button. Some organizations are segmenting their membership into groups, communicating more frequently to the most active members.

Urgency: By nature, an incoming e-mail ranks below a letter, a voicemail, and a fax in perceived importance. In an environment where nearly eighty percent of e-

mail is spam, the messages organizations send to their subscribers must be relevant, timely, and actionable. Experts in the field urge organizations to e-mail their members when something needs to be done right now. Demonstrate the need, and then provide a link that lets the subscriber take an immediate action.

Variety: When designing campaigns, whether for political or fund-raising purposes, wired organizations need to keep it fresh. As a constantly evolving medium, the internet rewards innovation and new ideas. Since many people skim their e-mail messages rather than read them word-for-word, a new kind of "ask" can jump out and grab the reader's attention. "Cool, I've never done that before!" can be a powerful motivator, and drive increased click-through rates.

Personality: Many of the most effective wired organizations develop a personal voice for their e-mail communications. Some larger groups, like MoveOn, have even developed multiple in-house personalities who are deployed on different campaigns. So a MoveOn member might receive a communication from founder Wes Boyd about one issue, and another e-mail from young standout Eli Pariser about a different MoveOn initiative.

With the "Name That Movie" contest coming to an end, it occurs to Jim that a "Save Evil Smiley" campaign could be the next promotional stunt to activate his e-subscribers and generate new ones. So Jim registers the URL "SaveEvilSmiley. com," and instant messages Jesse Haff, asking Jesse to create a webpage with the two posters side by side. Four hours later, Jesse's built a simple webpage featuring Robert's poster with the yellow-headed frown on the right, and a revised poster featuring yellow-headed Evil Smiley on the left. The mini-site includes an easy to use "send-to-a-friend" function, allowing visitors to automatically send a "Save Evil Smiley" message to five of their friends. To test-market the campaign, Jim e-mails the link around the office, seeking staff reaction.

The next day, the polls close for "Name That Movie," and Jim tallies up the 5,879 votes cast for the three titles and four subtitles. Incredibly, "Wal-Mart: The High Cost of Low Price" wins by a landslide, with over fifty percent of the votes. None of the alternate titles even come close. The public has spoken, and Robert's original title has been validated by his most passionate supporters.

The outcome is a bit of an anticlimax, but the "Name That Movie" process has been valuable in other ways. During the seven days of voting, hundreds of voters have signed up to host screenings during Wal-Mart Week. In fact, the title vote has been the most successful promotion Jim has devised to stir up enthusiasm among the membership and generate new screenings.

Later that afternoon, Robert announces the title during his hour-long live chat, while fielding questions from his fans and supporters. The last question of the live chat comes from a mysterious person named "B.J.," who voices a concern about the newly-unveiled poster art.

B.J.: "The 'logo' for this film would be much more effective if the 'smiley' was smiling. The current angry-face makes it look like a personal attack. People resent that, and then they instinctively reject what you are trying to say next."

Robert: "B.J., you've landed right smack in the middle of the battle within the Brave New Films electoral caucus. We've had extended debates, elaborate position papers, and a vir-

tual revolt among members of the caucus. Therefore, in the interest of pure democracy... and proof that we not only talk the talk, but walk the walk... Brave New Films now throws open the electoral college... the vote... I am deputizing Jim to create the infrastructure to have a vote on this issue. Stay tuned. And let the smiling begin."

Jim adds a triumphant note to the end of the chat: "WOOHOOOOO!!! Democracy rules... We're gonna get an up-or-down-vote on Evil Smiley!" The words "Evil Smiley" are a clickable link to SaveEvilSmiley.com, and within minutes people begin signing the online petition to Save Evil Smiley.

WAL*MART
the high cost of low price

Molding the Clay

In late June, Robert's four editors are pushing hard to prepare their segments for the first-ever assembly of an initial
rough cut. Doug Cheek and Jonathan Brock share the front
room during the day shift, each facing opposite walls and editing silently using headphones. The "night guy," Robert Florio,
comes in around 6:00 p.m., taking over Doug's workstation.

Chris Gordon, who has worked on all three of Robert's
documentaries, has his own adjoining private room with a
rare built-in air-conditioning unit. While the front room is
always overheated, due to the presence of two full-blown edit
stations, the back room that Chris inhabits is at least fifteen
degrees cooler.

Chris is in charge of the "Places" section, which is an
outgrowth of the Middlefield, Ohio story he has been cutting throughout the spring. This story of the demise of H&H
Hardware will now be followed by two newer stories from
Missouri and California. All three of the stories were produced by Caty.

Caty feels that her Missouri story may be the very best one she has produced. It has everything—sympathetic characters with regional flavor who articulate a powerful critique of the "Wal-Mart Effect." Irvin "Red" Esry, former owner of a four-store grocery chain, describes the way Wal-Mart obtained big subsidies from local government to build Supercenters in the Missouri towns of Cameron and Brookfield. Red claims that the subsidies, unavailable to him and other local shopkeepers, gave Wal-Mart an unfair competitive advantage in addition to the company's deep pockets and awesome purchasing power.

Chris has been spending the last week taking detailed notes on each of Caty's ten Missouri tapes. Using a Mac program called Notetaker,

Former grocery store owner Red Esry.

Chris writes down the gist of each soundbite, along with the corresponding timecode number. Chris' notes become the foundation of a story-writing effort that precedes the actual cutting of video.

On a smaller-scale documentary, Chris would be spending his days working side-by-side with the director. On a television-style production with multiple editors, Chris would be given a script by a segment producer or story producer, who would have already reviewed all the footage and composed an initial script by cutting and pasting favorite bits of dialogue from the transcripts.

Robert is open to employing story producers on a future project, but in general he prefers a compositional process based on looking at the footage rather than reading transcripts. "Picture and mood are so important in storytelling, and you can't

the high cost of low price

pick up those things from a transcript," he explains.

Without the involvement of a segment producer or story producer, the editors on the Retail Project play a primary role in composing the basic structure of each story. "Working this way gives me the most creative freedom I've ever experienced as an editor," explains Chris. "I get first crack at framing the story of each segment, and then I show Robert an initial rough cut. Robert has strong ideas about storytelling, and sometimes he tears my first cut apart frame by frame!" Robert likes to refer to his work in these initial edit sessions as "molding the clay."

On Friday, July 1, Robert arrives at the doorstep of the edit suite for an extended session with each of the three daytime editors. He's pushing hard for a first assembly of the movie that he can watch on July 4 while the rest of the staff enjoys a rare holiday break. Up until now, each segment has been edited and reviewed in isolation. With just two more months until he must "lock picture," Robert is hungry to get a feel for the overall arc of the film.

Robert's first stop is with Doug, who is reworking the "anti-union" segment that explores an attempt to unionize the auto service bay at a Wal-Mart in Loveland, Colorado. Loveland is one of Jenny's stories, and is one of the rare segments in which events unfolded in real time for the camera. The storytelling process for this segment is very different than for segments like Inglewood, which involve people's recollections of an event from the recent past.

Robert has a different rapport with each of his editors, and today's session with Doug is a passionate back-and-forth. Doug has strong ideas about what works and what doesn't, and sometimes he stands up and gestures at the computer screens to make a point.

The Loveland segment pits a young and naïve employee against an anti-union rapid response team sent out from Bentonville. "We're not yet selling the ominous nature of Wal-Mart's union-busting executives," Robert says. He suggests the possibility of using scary music, black-and-white images, or slow motion to add emotion to the sequence. "I don't know how to do that fancy stuff," huffs Doug, who seems to prefer a more naturalistic approach. "Maybe you'll be inspired when you recut the segment," Robert offers, raising the possibility of shooting a handful of close-ups showing hands on a steering wheel, gripping a cup of coffee, and other mundane activities. These inserts could be used as unsettling cutaways while the former managers describe Wal-Mart's anti-union procedures.

By turning his chair around 180 degrees and moving forward two feet, Robert has now departed Doug-world and entered Jonathan-world. There's only a narrow aisle between the back of Doug's chair and the back of Jonathan's chair, and yet both are able to concentrate completely, tuned into their headphones and monitors.

Robert is still getting to know Jonathan, who was brought on a month ago specifically to edit the opening of the movie and other high-energy, eye-catching segments. For the last month, Robert's idea has been to start the movie with an "up with Wal-Mart" montage, then make a brief homage to Sam Walton, and finally suggest that the company has gone sour since Walton's 1991 death. Jonathan's been cutting together footage from the small-town pageantry of thirty-nine store openings, creating a wholesome montage of marching bands, vocal groups, and ribbon cuttings.

Today Robert wants to know why Jonathan is taking so long to edit the opening sequence. "I'm dealing in flashing images," explains Jonathan. "I don't have a talker who might speak for half a minute or more." Robert wants the opening to be absolutely great, but he also has other segments to assign to Jonathan.

the high cost of low price

The director's final stop is the air-conditioned edit bay in the back, where Chris has a first cut of the Missouri segment ready for Robert to view. The mood in Chris' room is contemplative and subdued. Chris is a mellow, soft-spoken guy, and with the door closed and air conditioning running there's no sound from the outside world disturbing his flow.

Robert starts thinking out loud, talking through the potential order of the story points. There are long silences as Robert imagines the footage in different configurations. Like Doug, Chris has opinions about how to tell the story, but he expresses those ideas in a more gentle way, as if presenting possibilities for Robert to consider at his own pace.

Filmmaker's Toolbox:
Final Cut Pro

With the purchase of a MiniDV camera and a few microphones, an aspiring filmmaker can shoot footage at a very low cost. But until recently the high cost of editing video made it difficult and expensive to complete a documentary project.

The Avid editing system has been the industry-standard tool for editing video since the early 1990s. Requiring special hardware in addition to a Mac or PC, traditional Avid systems can cost well over $30,000 to purchase and more than $1,000 a week to rent. (Robert Greenwald Productions owns an Avid system that is used for Robert's scripted films and made-for-TV movies.)

Add the cost of an experienced freelance editor, and

the independent documentarian was burdened with an editing overhead of $8,000 or more per month. Enter Apple with a software-based editing system called Final Cut Pro, which requires no other hardware beyond a Macintosh computer and a standard external hard drive. Originally released in 1999, the easy-to-learn Final Cut Pro found an initial audience with wedding videographers and producers of corporate and industrial videos.

The release of the more powerful Final Cut Pro 3 in December of 2001 offered a new postproduction method for independent filmmakers with tight budgets. Rather than rent an Avid system and edit under time pressure, Morgan Spurlock purchased a Final Cut Pro 3 system to edit his $65,000 breakout hit *Super Size Me*. In fact, quite a few of the recent crop of successful documentaries were edited on Final Cut Pro, including *Spellbound, Gunner Palace, Control Room,* and *Murderball.* (During the same time period, Avid has introduced software-only products to compete against Apple in the low-end market.)

The cost difference between Final Cut Pro and the Avid hardware-based system has also attracted the interest of bigger budget filmmakers. Legendary film editor Walter Murch, best known for his work on *Apocalypse Now,* decided to use Final Cut Pro 3 on the $80 million film *Cold Mountain*. With the same money it would have cost to buy one Avid system, Murch deployed four networked Final Cut Pro systems on location in Romania. The multiple systems allowed assistant

the high cost of low price

editors to digitize footage, organize material, and create DVD "dailies" for the director without tying up Murch's personal edit station.

The Retail Project uses a similar "networked" approach, with seven Final Cut Pro HD systems in simultaneous operation. Three systems are full-blown edit stations that are used by Chris, Doug, Jonathan, and night editor Robert Florio. The four additional stations are used by the assistant editors and a rotating cast of unpaid interns, doing everything from digitizing incoming tapes to compressing and uploading QuickTime movies to the Wiki. All of the systems are connected via a high-speed network, so that footage and other audio/visual assets can be digitally transferred from one system to another.

In this particular edit session, Robert is deeply engaged in the compositional process, wrestling with the meaning and value of each soundbite. There are no incoming e-mails, no ringing phones, and no knocks on the door. The political and the personal come together ideally in this story," he exclaims. For sixty precious minutes, Robert has escaped the controlled chaos of his own making, and found sanctuary in Chris' comfortable, air-conditioned hideaway, entirely focused on "molding the clay."

Three days later, Robert is at home, watching the first rough cut of his Wal-Mart documentary at 5:00 a.m. on the July 4 holiday. The scene is a bit different than the way Francis Ford Coppola reviewed rough cuts of *Apocalypse Now*. There's no movie projector, no big screen, no test-audience of crewmembers, friends, and family. Not even any wine.

The "first viewing" of *Wal-Mart: The High Cost of Low Price* consists of Robert sitting in front of his PC, peering at a small QuickTime movie that measures about six inches across. He's selected this early-morning moment precisely because his family is still sleeping and everything is quiet. Rather than watching his first cut with others and gauging their reactions, Robert prefers a quiet, solo experience.

Last night, Robert started reading a new book by Malcolm Gladwell called *Blink*. Gladwell is a trendspotter best known for his book *The Tipping Point*. His new book describes the benefits of making snap decisions based on gut feeling and instinct. The book's premise, that our nonverbal hunches are often well-informed by complex experiences and memories, has reinforced Robert's convictions about his own process. In both hiring and editing, Robert likes to follow his instincts and go with his first impression.

Robert's first impression of the two-hour and seventeen minute rough cut is not good. His concept of dividing the film into "People" and "Places" sections just isn't working. Although the "People" and "Places" idea was only hatched a month ago, Robert feels it's time to reorganize the film once again. Although the segments will be moved around in relation to each other, Robert's primary goal of "pulling the audience into the personal stories" will not change.

After watching the rough cut from beginning to end, Robert starts reviewing the individual segments and taking notes. The family wakes up, breakfast is served, and Robert's still watching footage at his computer. You can hear the surf from Robert's house, but as the beach fills up with holiday sunbathers, Robert is still watching footage at the computer. Lunch is served, and Robert is still watching footage at the computer, a process that continues into the late afternoon.

At 9:45 a.m. the next morning, Robert presents the editorial staff with "Wal-Mart Movie Version 3.0." The film will

the high cost of low price

no longer begin with life as a Wal-Mart employee, expand to the impact of Wal-Mart on local communities, and then further expand to Wal-Mart's impact on other countries. Doug's "People" section of former Wal-Mart employees and managers will now be broken up into pieces, and these pieces will be distributed throughout the film. The order of the segments has been radically reworked.

Robert's new outline draws on subtle linkages between the various stories and characters, finding natural bridges between the last comment in one segment and the first words of another. As he tells the editors about the new sequence, Robert describes a theme for each transition, explaining the new order as a series of outros and intros.

After completing his rundown of the new script outline, Robert focuses the group on the opening of the film. He's now convinced that the main characters must be introduced at the very top. Referring once again to *The Towering Inferno,* Robert reminds the group that his film can be thought of as a "disaster movie," where an ensemble cast is introduced before the disaster strikes. For the first time, Robert gives the crew a list of ten people he thinks will be the main characters of the film. Although this information is received quietly by the editors, it feels like a breakthrough. After a five-month shoot that produced almost 350 hours of original footage, ten characters have emerged as the "stars" of the film.

Robert suggests that the editors, assistant editors, and co-producers each pull their favorite "character-establishing" sound bites for the ten "stars." These bites do not have to reference Wal-Mart at all. They simply need to offer a glimpse into the individuality of each person. Robert gives his team three days to gather the material, so that Doug will have an inventory of "character establishing" bites to play with later this week.

Curiously, Robert has assigned the character-establishing

project to Doug rather than Jonathan, who up until now has been responsible for the opening. Jonathan has been assigned a newly-conceived montage of abandoned main streets. This new moody section will be used as a transitional piece after the closing of H&H Hardware in Middlefield.

"I do the touchy-feely montage stuff that will be peppered in throughout the film," explains Jonathan, who is unruffled by losing control of the opening. "The more editing that happens, the more clarity Robert gets. It's all about helping the man crystallize his idea," says Jonathan.

On the other side of the room, Doug's in a self-described "flopsweat" looking for soundbites that can be used to introduce the three former store managers. "I'm just not finding the stuff I expected to be there," he grumbles.

Robert's Independence Day restructuring has hit Doug hardest regarding his Jonquiere, Canada segment. "I spent a long time on the story of a Wal-Mart store that was closed down after the employees successfully voted to unionize," Doug explains. "Now Robert wants to blend this story into the other international material. I didn't have the heart to tear up my own work, but it kind of upsets me to know that Florio will be sitting in this chair carving up my segment later tonight."

WAL★MART
the high cost of low price

😈 Crime

On July 8, after five full months of shooting, Robert Greenwald is finally about to conduct an interview himself. Kristy and Sarah are setting up camera and lights at the Beverly Hills law offices of Gary Dordick. Gary and his client Laura Tanaka are due to show up any minute now, and Robert wants to be able to roll tape within minutes of Laura's arrival.

Robert expects the interview to be difficult, and wants everything handled with maximum sensitivity. Laura has been flown in to speak on camera about something that happened to her in a Wal-Mart parking lot. Robert has been pursuing crime stories for months now, and it has been very hard to find a crime victim willing to go through the pain of re-living her experience on camera.

When Gary's BMW pulls into the parking lot, Robert tells the crew he wants to get Laura wired for sound and into her interview chair as quickly as possible. Robert then positions himself at the doorway of the office where the interview will be filmed, ready to greet Laura when she comes up the stairs.

Laura arrives, dressed in casual California style, wearing a flowered scoop-neck top, jeans, and fashionable platform shoes. She looks more like someone heading to an upscale mall than a crime victim going to her attorney's office to be videotaped.

Robert shakes her hand, and smiles. "Thank you very much for coming all this way, we really appreciate you being here," he says softly. "We're going to talk for a little while. The camera turns on and off, and if at the end there's something you're not comfortable with, then we don't have to use it," he explains.

Laura Tanaka, who was kidnapped from a Wal-Mart parking lot.

A tiny lavalier microphone is clipped onto Laura's blouse, connected by a thin cable to a transmitter box she puts in her pocket. Laura and Robert sit facing each other on Gary's high-backed upholstered chairs, while Kristy makes a few quick adjustments to the lighting.

Without any announcement that tape is rolling, Kristy puts the camera into record. Robert begins by asking Laura to tell him her full name, and where she lives. He then serves up some easy questions to make her comfortable. Laura tells Robert about her current job, and how long she's lived out of state. One reason she left California is that one of the two men who "carjacked" her is due to be paroled soon, and she expects he will return to the same community where she used to live. She doesn't want to be living there when he gets out of jail.

Robert asks Laura about the lawsuit she filed against Wal-Mart. She explains that for the first two weeks after the crime took place, she was afraid to leave her apartment. She was

WAL★MART
the high cost of low price

paralyzed with fear that the men who attacked her would re-appear at her home. They'd taken her driver's license, so they knew where she lived.

Feeling like she had lost control of her life, Laura started doing internet research about crime in Wal-Mart parking lots. She wondered if other shoppers had been through a similar experience. What she found startled her: A substantial amount of crime was occurring in Wal-Mart parking lots, and yet the company's security effort was almost entirely focused on protecting the merchandise inside the stores rather than the customers outside the stores.

The more Laura found out about Wal-Mart's security, the more she felt that the crime she suffered could have been pre-vented. Although she told Robert that it's impossible to elimi-nate all crime, she felt that Wal-Mart had not taken the basic and reasonable safety precautions customers expect from a national retailer.

Laura and Robert have been cautiously circling around the crime itself. Finally Robert zeros in on the heart of the in-terview. "Would you feel comfortable telling us a little about what happened to you that night?" Robert asks tentatively. Laura nods, purses her lips, and says OK.

"I was going to Wal-Mart to return some blinds," she be-gins after a pause, leading Robert and his crew down her har-rowing journey. Laura parked four spaces from the front door, between a van and a pickup with a camper shell. "When I got out, there were two of them," she recounts. "They just blocked me in and I couldn't get away. He said he had a knife at that point. I found out later he had a gun."

Laura tried giving them the keys. The men said they didn't want the keys, and didn't want the car. "They told me to get in the car," she says, and feeling like she had no other choice, she did as she was told.

Robert asks Laura what was going through her mind at

this point. She says she remembered a safety presentation given to her and other employees at a recent job. "They had the insurance department out there and they were talking about, if you're in a parking lot and this happens, don't go with 'em. If you go with 'em you're probably not going to live. Statistically, that's what happens. They'll kill you. I thought they were going to rape me, too."

Laura continues her story, explaining how she jumped out of the car as it passed by a gas station. "I decided if they're going to kill me I want to choose where this happens. You hear all these stories about people not being found." When one of her assailants produced a gun, Laura reluctantly got back in the car. "You go kind of cold inside," she says. "I just kind of resigned that there was nothing I could do."

When Laura was driven to a remote rural area, she feared the worst. "They made me undo my top, expose myself. It was almost like he got disgusted with himself and then let me go. Even after they let me go, I thought it was some kind of game." Laura hid for a while behind some trees, before seeking refuge in a nearby farmhouse. "A very kind woman ended up calling the police," she says, marking the end of her ordeal.

Laura's recounting of the crime has unfolded over the course of five minutes, and it's some of the most powerful footage Robert and his co-producers have collected. Robert asked only two or three questions during this five-minute period, because once Laura got started talking about the crime, the words just kept tumbling out.

The interview comes to a natural end about ten minutes later. Robert asks Laura if she plans to enjoy Los Angeles for a few hours before her flight home. She replies with a smile, "Actually, I'd like to see how Gary does in his turn in the hot seat."

So Kristy and Sarah move the camera and lights into Gary's office while Robert chats with Laura. The antecham-

the high cost of low price

ber to Gary's office is lined with framed newspaper clippings of his achievements as a personal injury lawyer. The photo in the article about legal heavyweights under forty shows Gary in workout clothes looking like a *Men's Health* model.

Gary takes a seat behind his large wooden desk, and asks if any of his knickknacks are in the way of Kristy's shot. One of these items Kristy asks him to remove is a small plastic brain, which he tosses on the floor. There are larger models of the human brain on a credenza behind his desk. "I do a lot of head injury cases," he explains.

During his brief interview, Gary gives Robert a behind-the-scenes look at how difficult it is to sue Wal-Mart. According to Gary, the company concedes nothing and offers maximum resistance at every stage. When he confronted Wal-Mart with the fact that they had two hundred video cameras inside the store where Laura was abducted, and not a single camera outside, Gary was stunned by the company's response. "They said some of the cameras inside the store are fake," he exclaims.

Laura's case against Wal-Mart hinged, in part, on internal company documents that were extraordinarily difficult to obtain. "They just don't respect the discovery process," Gary says, citing a widely-publicized case involving a similar kidnapping in Texas. After being abducted at a Wal-Mart parking lot and then raped, Donna Meissner sued Wal-Mart for failing to provide proper security. Wal-Mart's resistance to providing the documents requested by Meissner's attorney was so extreme that district court judge James Mehaffy fined the company eighteen million dollars. "Not only in this court but in other courts [Wal-Mart] has demonstrated a clear pattern of desiring to flaunt the rules, to hide, to cheat, to give false answers under oath," said the judge, angry that Wal-Mart had suppressed a 1993 internal study on crime in their parking lots. "The fact that they concealed something of that magnitude is, standing alone, evidence of their intent to conceal."

The scope of Wal-Mart's legal resources is enormous. According to a legal industry publication, the company spends over $200 million a year on services provided by one hundred different law firms. Between the company's hardball approach and deep pockets, Wal-Mart may be the toughest adversary a plaintiff's attorney can ever face.

Although it took years, Laura won her case, and it was upheld when Wal-Mart appealed. After years of effort, Gary won $500,000 for his client. "From a financial perspective, this kind of case is a money loser for an attorney," Gary tells Robert. "The amount of time and effort it takes to sue a company like this costs far more than what you can recover in legal fees. But I'd take another case like this again in a minute," he says with a smile.

Later, Robert reflects on the ethics of interviewing crime victims. Getting good material is important, but showing respect and kindness to the crime victim is even more important. "We have to wear our film hat and our human hat," he says.

WAL★MART
the high cost of low price

Making Contact

On Tuesday, July 12, Robert decides it's finally time to reach out to Bentonville and ask for an interview with Wal-Mart CEO Lee Scott. Dialing the main number for corporate headquarters, Robert asks for Lee Scott's office, and leaves a message that he is making a documentary film about Wal-Mart and is inviting Scott to participate.

Intern Paris Marron is videotaping Robert as he makes this call from his desk. In the public relations battles to come, it might be useful to have proof that Robert did in fact offer Wal-Mart a chance to put Lee Scott on camera.

A few hours later, the staff gathers in Robert's office for the Tuesday afternoon weekly meeting. The first order of business is Lee Scott. Robert tells the staff about the message he left this morning, and announces a new assignment for his already up-to-the-hilt-in-work crew.

"I want each of you to call the Wal-Mart main office on a different day while being videotaped by Paris," Robert says. "Ask for Lee Scott's office, and tell whoever answers the phone that you are working on the movie and it's very important to you that Scott appears on camera. Feel free to personalize your plea—tell them about your particular job, and why you think it would be great for Lee Scott to have a chance to say his piece about Wal-Mart."

Robert gleefully explains that at the end of this process, he'll be able to create a wonderful montage of different staffers trying to convince Wal-Mart to participate in the documentary. Whether this footage is used in the actual film, in advertising, or on the website, it should be a priceless addition to Robert's media arsenal.

The staff is abuzz with questions. What if they ask us about the content of the film? How much are we allowed to say?

Robert begins to answer, and is interrupted by his desk phone, which beeps. Robert's receptionist comes on the speakerphone. "Lee Scott on the line for you," she says blandly, as if he's just another Joe Schmo. "I'll take it," exclaims Robert.

Without instruction, the staffers get out of their seats and gather around Robert's L-shaped desk. A hush descends on the room as Paris rushes over to the camera, which is already on a tripod in the corner. When it's perfectly quiet, Paris signals that she's ready.

Robert picks up the receiver with a simple "Hello." There's a pause while Robert listens to the caller.

"Speaking."

Robert's tone is measured, as if he's choosing his words carefully.

"I'm very well."

"I did."

"We're making a movie about Wal-Mart and I wanted to give Mr. Scott the opportunity to come on camera and comment."

The staff lets out a collective silent sigh. It's not actually

Lee Scott on the phone, but one of his minions. The volume on Robert's handset is so low that the staff can't even tell the gender of the person on the other end of the line.

"So you're the head of Communications?"

Robert's tone has lightened, and is now congenial.

"Congratulations. That must be an interesting job these days," he says with a mild undercurrent of sarcasm.

The research staff has read so much about Wal-Mart that they instantly know who is on the line: Mona Williams, Wal-Mart VP of Corporate Communications. The handful of staffers who brought laptops to the meeting immediately run a Google search on Mona.

Mona seems to be floating the idea of including someone else from Wal-Mart in the film instead of Lee Scott.

"I don't want to be difficult about this, but I think it is incredibly important that it be Mr. Scott. If he does it and then he says, 'Well, I would also think in the interest of fairness, you should talk to so and so,' we'd also be happy to do that."

"Our timeframe is the next couple of weeks."

"Well, it's hard to show somebody in a negative light. You know film can't put words in anybody's mouth. And film can't make you behave in any particular way."

"No, no. I'm from New York. It's basically impossible for you to insult me."

The staff likes that one, looking around and smiling at each other.

The conversational tone has become increasingly stylized, as Robert's demeanor shifts into a patronizing Hollywood jiveness. It's almost like a superhero's first encounter with his archnemesis. Batman meets the Joker. Luke meets Darth. The scene in a Western when a gunslinger drawls "There's a new Sheriff in town." The rivals size each other up, knowing that the next time they meet will be in battle.

Suddenly Robert laughs into the phone.

"You're *good* at your job," he says, voice dripping with sarcasm. Robert laughs again.

"If I were to give you all the issues we are addressing in the film now, before you told me Mr. Scott wanted to be in the movie, it actually wouldn't be too smart of me."

"It was a very good try. I almost fell for it, too! Very smooth."

"So when you stop working for Wal-Mart, maybe you want to come work on movies?"

"You would have a very successful career in Hollywood if you came here."

"Great. Thank You. Bye."

Robert hangs up the phone.

"Ooooh, she's gooooood," he says, milking the line. Everybody laughs and claps, releasing the pent-up tension of twenty people who were absolutely silent during a fascinating moment in the history of the project.

The next day, a one-paragraph e-mail from Mona arrives, declining the opportunity to have Lee Scott interviewed for the film. Attached to Mona's e-mail is a screenshot of the main page of WalMartMovie.com, which she oddly refers to as a "flyer." According to her e-mail, the word "evil" was the deciding factor in Lee Scott's decision not to participate. Conceived by Jim just a few weeks earlier, the "Save Evil Smiley" campaign is already resonating at the home office in Bentonville.

Robert decides that the whole exchange is too much fun to cut off so soon, and places a call to Mona, who is in a meeting. She calls Robert back on the same day, July 13. Robert tells Mona he was very disappointed to get her e-mail. Mona immediately focuses on the "flyer." She's still bent out of shape about Evil Smiley.

Again, Paris is videotaping Robert as he talks to Mona on the phone. Sarah and Jim are also in the office, witnessing Robert's side of the brief conversation.

"What if we posted your interview online," Robert asks. "The full text of your interview so that I couldn't distort it."

No dice. Mona's not budging. Robert ends the call with a promise to send Mona a box set of his documentaries on DVD.

Later in the day, Robert posts an account of his conversations with Mona on his blog. He offers a comment from Mona that presages the battle to come.

"When November comes, we will be very aggressive in getting our side of the story out. We will do it separately where we can control what we say and how it's presented."

Aggressive. Control. The two words describe Robert's corporate adversary as well as any interview with Lee Scott ever could.

WAL★MART
the high cost of low price

Welding the Arc

Since his four editors are already maxed-out with work, Robert decides to hire a fifth editor for the China footage. Night editor Robert Florio suggests a friend, Jessica, who meets Robert, Kerry, and Sarah on July 15 to discuss a potentially huge assignment. Not only does Robert want a seven- to ten-minute China segment for his film, but he also wants an extended thirty- to forty-minute version that can be used as bonus material for the DVD or made available at WalMart-Movie.com.

Everyone in the meeting agrees that the China segment should be dubbed rather than subtitled, to help make an emotional connection with the main character, a young Chinese woman who assembles toys in Shenzhen Province that are sold by Wal-Mart in the US. As always, Robert is insistent that the character be established early in the segment. He wants the viewer to becomes invested in her individual story before raising the broader issue of the unseen human cost of "Every Day Low Prices."

There's just one problem: Jessica's not available to start until the end of July, and the China segment is one of Robert's top priorities. So Robert decides to hold off making a decision on what to do with China until his four editors have a chance to work through their current assignments. If Florio's encounter with the Laura Tanaka crime footage goes smoothly, perhaps he'll free up sooner than expected and be able to take on the China segment.

China's not the only thing Robert has on his mind at the moment. He continues to tinker with the overall structure of the film, watching a new assembly each weekend in search of the perfect sequence.

Robert's struggle with the segment order is a solitary effort, but nobody on the staff could accuse him of being parochial or secretive about his creative process. Robert publishes regular script updates to the entire staff, and talks through creative issues during the weekly Tuesday staff meeting. All of the footage is available on the Wiki, along with every version of the individual segments and each of the weekly rough cuts.

Yet Robert hasn't sought out much feedback from his staff. "At this point, I need to get my vision down before I entertain other smart, creative ideas," he says. "When I have my sculpture in place, then I welcome the comments and input."

Jim is the one person who makes sure to watch each new cut and give feedback to Robert via e-mail. "I send Robert a small handful of notes whenever I watch cuts. All of my notes tend to be around framing and potential areas we'll get attacked on," explains Jim.

Overall, there's very little dialogue among the staff about the movie as a whole. Meeting the September 3 deadline to "lock picture" puts a tremendous weight on everybody, and the workload has effectively compartmentalized the filmmaking process.

the high cost of low price

The editors, who pass by each other's stations multiple times a day, can't take time out to watch and discuss their collective works. Even the assistant editors who actually build the rough cuts in Final Cut Pro don't have time to watch them. "You end up missing a bit of that 'movie magic' feeling," says assistant editor Lissette Roldan with a sigh as she uses a drag-and-drop process to assemble the next rough cut.

Meanwhile, Robert toils with the story arc, continuing to move segments around in search of the magic combination. On July 16, Robert publishes a new script outline that returns in large part to his original script, minus the "Current Employee" section. The demise of H&H Hardware in Middlefield is once again moved up to the front, and the triumphant victory of Inglewood is returned to its original position near the end. Like the original script, this new version radiates outward from Middle America, moving from Ohio to Missouri to the West Coast, then to Canada, Europe, and Asia.

"The basic concept, to start with the specific, the human and then build to the pattern, the systemic, is beginning to work very well," says Robert in his e-mail to the staff. "Florio calls it 'the tip of the iceberg approach,' and that's a good one-liner to keep in mind."

Filmmaker's Toolbox:
Balancing the Creative and the Political

In traditional Hollywood, directors are constantly struggling with the delicate act of "balancing art and commerce." Yet Robert sees a totally different challenge in his documentary work, namely balancing art and politics. Editing a political documentary presents a series of key decision points in which either the creative or the political must be favored, and the overall sum of those decisions has huge implications.

"You don't want to make an infomercial or a polemic," says Robert. "As a filmmaker, you want to tell a story in an engaging and entertaining way. But sometimes the basic rules of moviemaking need to be bent or broken in order to effectively deliver your political argument."

A classic example is the beginning of Robert's first documentary, *Uncovered*. One of the most basic rules of entertainment is to grab the interest of your viewers at the very beginning of a film. Yet for *Uncovered*, Robert chose to start the film with each of the experts introducing themselves and saying a word about their years of experience in intelligence or diplomacy. "Who in their right mind would start a movie with twenty-five people introducing themselves?" Robert asks rhetorically. Yet for this particular movie, the political won out over the creative. Operating in an environment where the mainstream media were firmly in support of the Iraq war, Robert decided to establish "unimpeachable credibility" at the very top.

Robert's e-mail also contains some big news: He's planning a pair of screenings for the end of the month. The July 27 "internal" screening will be for staffers only, to be followed a week later by an "external" screening for invited guests and friends of the project. It seems that the director is finally ready to formally ask for feedback on his work-in-progress. With the external screening planned for August 4, there will be just five weeks of editing remaining to polish up the movie

the high cost of low price

before "locking picture" in early September.

One week later, Robert's in the editing room with Florio, going over the crime segment. Over the past few days, Florio's created a powerful and disturbing piece. Beginning with Laura Tanaka's harrowing account, the segment continues with a montage of news clips about similar crimes that have taken place all over the country. What looks at first like a single, horrific occurrence is shown to be part of a larger pattern of neglect and possible negligence, leaving the viewer angry at Wal-Mart's disregard for the safety of their employees and customers.

The crime segment has come together so quickly that Robert decides to give Florio the China assignment, which he starts in the last week of July. Working from the English-language transcripts, Florio uses a highlighter to mark the bits

Chinese workers outside toy factory in Shenzhen province.

of dialogue that look most promising, and pulls the corresponding videoclips. He then asks Lissette to serve as a "voice double," recording the Chinese workers' dialogue in English. Once each clip has Lissette's dub track attached, Florio can edit the segment as if the footage was shot in English rather than Chinese. Florio quickly becomes attached to the story of the young factory worker and her boyfriend, saying "there's almost an entire movie in this footage!"

On July 26, a day before the internal screening was supposed to take place, Robert is still reworking his script outline. He'd hoped to have the structure fully in place by this point, but he has not yet been able to solve the puzzle. The internal screening has been pushed back for three to five days, maybe more.

The good news is that the individual segments are getting stronger and stronger. Robert's been applying the "tip of the iceberg" approach to each individual segment, and he's loving the results. "We're trying to start each section in the smallest, most personal place," he explains, holding up his two index fingers an inch apart. "You get to know a person, you learn their story, and then at the end of the segment you find out there are dozens of communities where Wal-Mart has done the same thing."

Beyond its effectiveness in making emotional connections with the viewer, the "tip of the iceberg" approach hammers home the idea that each of Wal-Mart's various misdeeds are part of a broader pattern of corporate misbehavior, rather than the work of a few bad apples.

As the segments get stronger and pack an increasingly emotional payoff, they are now competing with each other for prime position within the film. "We are even starting to dial down the intensity of a few segments that appear in the first half, so that we don't overplay our hand too early," Robert explains.

Balancing the unfolding political argument, the emotional arc, and the many transitions between segments has become a bit like scheduling the NFL season. Yet while the NFL has a team of experts and fancy computers to solve their annual Rubik's Cube, Robert is relying solely on his gut instinct and a notebook stuffed with handwritten diagrams.

WAL★MART
the high cost of low price

☺ Theatrical Release

On July 15, Robert convenes the Brave New Films team for a brainstorming session about adding a theatrical release to the November campaign. Independent film distribution companies don't want to touch Robert's new movie, for fear of offending Wal-Mart, the number one seller of movies on DVD. So the group is exploring the idea of putting together a limited New York and Los Angeles theatrical run without the involvement of a distribution company.

Clustered together on the L-shaped couch in Robert's office, Jim, Lisa, Devin, and Sarah are peering at photocopies of a profit-and-loss projection. It's the first time a spreadsheet has appeared in one of these meetings, and everyone in the room is having trouble understanding it.

The spreadsheet details the cost of presenting the Wal-Mart film for a four-week commercial run at one theater in New York and one theater in Los Angeles. Robert is the only person in the room who is familiar with the Byzantine deal structure of a theatrical release, and even he is having trouble coming to grips with the numbers. If the spreadsheet is correct, a simple two-city theatrical run is going to cost nearly $35,000 and would almost definitely be a money-losing endeavor for Brave New Films.

As the group talks through the mechanics of traditional independent film distribution, the limitations of "old media" become all too clear. For decades, art house theater owners have depended on "exclusivity" to get the best return from films with niche appeal. Exclusivity is designed to strictly limit the ways and places that a particular movie can be seen.

First, entertainment industry convention dictates that a movie must not be available on television or DVD until several months after its theatrical run. This "exclusive theatrical window" ensures that the most motivated viewers buy a full-priced movie ticket. Secondly, the owner of an art house theater usually demands an exclusive engagement within a certain geographic area. On *Outfoxed,* for example, the Quad Cinema had the exclusive engagement for all of Manhattan.

Filmmaker's Toolbox:
Documentaries at the Box Office

The invention of digital video and the DVD have combined to make it much more affordable to produce and distribute documentary films. Yet documentaries are still an insignificant sliver of movie theater revenue. Only four documentaries have ever grossed more than ten million dollars in US theaters, and only fifteen have passed the three million mark.

The one bona-fide megahit in the history of docu-

the high cost of low price

mentary is Michael Moore's *Fahrenheit 9/11*, which grossed $119 million in the summer of 2004. The film became "forbidden fruit" when the Walt Disney Company refused to distribute it several months earlier. Bought back from Disney by Miramax founders Bob and Harvey Weinstein, *Fahrenheit 9/11* was released through independents Lion's Gate Pictures and IFC Films. Debuting in 868 theaters, the film generated so much interest that Lion's Gate and IFC were able to expand it to 2011 theaters, an unheard-of "wide release" for a documentary film. Generating massive international publicity, *Fahrenheit 9/11* grossed an additional $100 million outside the US.

While the box office numbers for other documentaries are miniscule compared to *Fahrenheit 9/11*, there's been a surge of successful releases in the wake of Moore's earlier hit, *Bowling for Columbine*. Grossing $21.5 million, *Columbine* shattered the previous documentary box office record of $7.7 million that was set by *Hoop Dreams* in 1994. *Columbine* was also a major hit on DVD, introducing a new generation of movie fans to the documentary genre and paving the way for a number of subsequent films, including *Fahrenheit 9/11*.

From *Columbine*'s October 2002 release through June 2005, ten documentary films exceeded $3 million in theatrical box office, including the $11.5 million breakout success of *Super Size Me*. A scathing critique of McDonald's, *Super Size Me* demonstrates that anti-corporate films are some of the most profitable documentaries at the multiplex. *Super Size Me,* Moore's first film *Roger and Me,* and *Enron: The Smartest Guys in the Room* are three of the all-time top ten documentary films at the box office, each shining a spotlight on one of America's biggest corporations.

Outfoxed grossed $405,900 in a limited run at eighteen theaters in August 2004, and *Uncovered* grossed $190,424 in a shorter run just a few weeks later. The movie business evaluates these limited runs based on the average gross "per screen," and by this measure *Outfoxed* was a significant success, breaking the all-time single-week box-office record at New York's Quad Cinemas. The "per screen" numbers generated by *Outfoxed* are especially impressive considering the fact that the movie was already available on DVD and had been seen for free at thousands of house parties in the month prior to its theatrical release.

Few documentaries ever get a commercial release beyond the tastemaker markets of New York and Los Angeles, and many important documentaries find their audience on television networks like PBS, HBO, and the BBC without any kind of theatrical run.

These two forms of exclusivity drive all interested viewers within a market to one or two movie theaters, maximizing revenue by eliminating any potential competition. Usually there is no other way to see the movie until several months later when the DVD is released.

Advertising an exclusive art house run can require a

the high cost of low price

small fortune in a top media market like New York or Los Angeles, where tiny ads in the newspaper can cost thousands of dollars. According to the spreadsheet prepared for today's meeting, a modest ten-day print ad campaign for the first week of a New York engagement would cost the Retail Project almost $13,000. Expand the plan to a two-week run in New York and Los Angeles, and the advertising cost balloons to $26,000.

Distributors of big-budget movies take out much larger print ads and spend millions of dollars on television spots, but are able to amortize the cost over many theaters within each market. Yet the limited audience for independent films makes theater owners wary of competing with each other. So the distributor of an independent film faces the highest cost structure in the industry: buying high-priced ads in the nation's most expensive media markets to support just a handful of revenue-generating engagements.

Coming from a dotcom background, Jim is astounded, even offended by the cost of the proposed two-city theatrical plan. "We could do so much with that money," he says, shaking his head. "And what are we going to say to our thousands of screening hosts? We've been telling them for months that *they* are going to premiere the movie during Wal-Mart Week!"

Suddenly old media and new media are in direct conflict. Robert's been advised that theater owners will only book the Wal-Mart film if they have an exclusive window before the house parties, to avoid competing with hundreds of free showings. Yet a four-week theatrical run in advance of Wal-Mart Week could deflate much of the excitement among the grass-roots organizations and individual house party hosts.

"Why not debut the movie during Wal-Mart Week, get a ton of publicity, and then have the theater owners beg us for a theatrical run," demands Jim loudly. "That's what happened with *Outfoxed*, we did the house parties first and *then* the theatrical release."

Robert motions for Jim to settle down. "My thinking is that a limited theatrical run in New York and LA could help generate some of the initial press, setting up Wal-Mart Week to be an even bigger deal. Maybe we trim it down to just one or two weeks in the beginning of November, leading right into Wal-Mart Week," he offers.

"But do we even *need* a theatrical release at all," moans Jim. "We've invented a new way to present our movie, bypassing the lame old ways."

Sarah, who has been quiet thus far, raises a crucial point. "No matter how few people actually see the movie in a theater, a theatrical release still gives a special sheen that makes our documentary a *movie* rather than a *video*."

There's a pause, as everyone nods in agreement. Beyond the prestige, there's the question of precedent. Both *Uncovered* and *Outfoxed* had theatrical releases, with *Outfoxed* in particular generating some pretty respectable numbers in New York. Would the absence of a theatrical release for *Wal-Mart: The High Cost of Low Price* make the new campaign seem like a step backward?

Robert proposes a way to move forward. "How about we pencil in a New York world-premiere on Thursday, November 3, with a ten-day New York and LA theatrical run starting Friday the 4th. The theatrical run ends on Sunday, November 12, which is the first night of Wal-Mart Week."

"I can live with it," Jim says, closing his laptop with a flourish, and the meeting breaks.

"That was productive," Robert says in an encouraging tone of voice, as he stands up from his chair. "Payyynful," mutters Jim under his breath.

☺ Still Growing

On the morning of Sunday, July 31, Robert watches a new rough cut at home on his computer. With the addition of the newly-edited "China" and "Crime" segments, the running time has ballooned by almost a half-hour, clocking in at two hours, forty-five minutes, and twenty seconds.

Tomorrow will be August 1, which drives home the hard truth that Robert has just one more month to complete the creative process and "lock picture." The internal screening, originally scheduled for July 27, has been pushed back twice and may need to be postponed again. "Normally, I'd want six months to polish and finish this film," Robert says, "but we have only thirty-three days." With a goal of delivering a ninety-minute finished product, Robert will need to cut out over an hour of material in the next four and a half weeks.

The trimming process has been made even more difficult because important new footage continues to be shot. According to Lissette, the total number of original hours of footage grew from 301 at the beginning of July to 361 at the beginning of August. Robert's been intimately involved with the newest material, which includes Laura Tanaka's crime interview and two other key interviews that were also conducted locally by Robert himself.

Rather than feeling bogged down by the influx of new material, Robert is upbeat about the late additions. "Everything we shot in July was based on a need I saw within one of the segments. Instead of pursuing new issues, we're strengthening the stories that are already in the film. In many cases the questions I'm asking in these interviews are very specific, aiming to fill in gaps and flesh out key story points."

On August 1, Robert convenes a morning meeting of the editors, to go through his notes on the lengthy new rough cut. As Robert moves from segment to segment, his comments are focused on how to make each segment stronger rather than shorter. One particular segment, on how Wal-Mart affects the overall jobs picture in the US, is likely to be expanded. "From a purely creative standpoint, the jobs segment is something we would cut out right about now," Robert tells the editors. "We just didn't find characters strong enough to make this segment competitive with our best stories. Yet Wal-Mart is always talking about how many jobs they create when they open a new store, and it's imperative from a political standpoint to refute them."

Robert's comment begins a short brainstorming session where the editors suggest various soundbites that might be helpful in building up the jobs segment. At this point, only the Wiki itself can remember every interview and every topic. Each person in the room has a familiarity with only a subset of the 361 hours of original footage that's been shot.

The process of trimming the overall running time of the film has not yet begun. Robert does refer to it as a challenge that's coming soon. "I think there's twenty to thirty minutes

the high cost of low price

that are easy to cut out," he predicts. "After that, it's going to get tough."

The meeting breaks, and each editor heads back to his station with an assignment to refine one or two particular segments. The assistant editors walk back to their overheated room, and are greeted by co-producer Kerry Candaele, who has just returned from interviewing the family and friends of murder victim Megan Holden in Texas. A nineteen-year-old college student and Wal-Mart associate, Megan was abducted from a Wal-Mart parking lot at the end of her evening shift in January 2005.

"Can I watch the new rough cut?" inquires Kerry tentatively. "Sure," replies Lissette, warning him that it's over two and a half hours. Kerry sits in front of one of the Final Cut Pro systems, and starts watching the same six-inch wide Quick-Time movie that Robert viewed twenty-four hours earlier.

British produce vendor Neil Stockwell.

Within the first fifteen minutes, Kerry's feeling a bit overwhelmed. "There's so many stories, so much stuff!" he remarks to nobody in particular. A moment later, Kerry's London segment comes up, and he's delighted that one of his favorite characters is featured, a cockney-accented fruit-seller who is teaming up with his fellow open-air merchants to resist the replacement of their bazaar with a shiny new Wal-Mart.

Checking his watch, Kerry realizes he doesn't have another two hours to stay here and watch the entire cut, so he decides to skip ahead to the China segment. Kerry's never seen a rough edit of his China footage, and is eager to find out how it's coming together.

When the segment starts, Kerry realizes that the main

character is being voiced in English by Lissette, who is sitting right next to him. Kerry reaches out to pat Lissette on the back, saying "That sounds great! I didn't know you did Chinese!" Lissette replies with a smile, "I don't do Chinese, only Chinese-accent." In fact Lissette is Colombian, and has applied a tentative "English-is-my-second language" gloss to her dub track that avoids any particular national flavor.

As the China segment unfolds, Kerry's concerned that a lot of interesting story-points are missing. "I'm worried that it's boring and doesn't go anywhere," Kerry says. Yet he has no plans to work directly with Florio on polishing the segment. "I'm not a filmmaker. I've never done this before," Kerry says quietly. "It's a very difficult process."

Listening in from across the room, Mobolaji encourages Kerry to stay engaged with the editorial process. "As long as your comments are on point with the story Robert wants to tell, I think they are legit," he advises. Kerry nods, and the China segment ends. Looking at his watch, Kerry packs up his bag and says his goodbyes. But instead of turning left at the courtyard towards the main entrance, Kerry turns right, heading to the edit suites.

Next door to the assistant editor's room, Jim has been reviewing the results of an online poll. After a month of intensive R&D, the "send-to-a-friend" DVD idea is finally ready to be market-tested by the house party hosts, and the response has been quite positive.

Conceived by marketing guru Seth Godin six weeks earlier in a conference call with Robert, Jim, Rick, and Lisa, the "send-to-a-friend" concept has been renamed the "DVD Screamer." Sarah came up with this nickname in last week's Brave New Films meeting, a play-on-words referencing the DVD "screeners" that are sent to Academy Award voters each year. The DVD Screamer would be packaged in a ready-to-mail cardboard envelope, complete with postage. Jim has been col-

laborating with Seth via e-mail on refining the Screamer concept for the past several weeks.

According to the current plan, hosts of Wal-Mart Week screenings would encourage their attendees to buy a Screamer or two as a way to share the movie with family and friends. After paying the host five dollars for a Screamer, an attendee would fill in the "to" and "from" areas on the outside of the package. Either the host or the attendee would drop the post-paid Screamer in a mailbox the next morning, creating a fast-moving viral spread of the movie and its message.

Seventy-five percent of house party hosts who respond to Jim's survey say the DVD Screamer is "definitely" a good idea, and almost ninety-three percent say that they would definitely or probably include the DVD Screamer as part of their house party. Jim and Seth are so excited about the DVD Screamer that they wonder if, one year from now, the send-to-a-friend DVD will become a standard part of the media activist's toolkit.

Across the courtyard, Lisa and Devin are having second thoughts about how the DVD Screamer fits into the multiple distribution channels that have already been put in place. One of Lisa's most powerful appeals when talking to nonprofits and other organizations is the usefulness of the full-price DVD as a fund-raising tool. She's worried that organizations will view the five-dollar Screamer as a low-priced competitor to the standard DVDs that organizations will be selling to their members for $12.95, $14.95, or even $19.95.

Devin has a similar concern about the possibility that the DVD Screamer could cannibalize commercial sales of the standard DVD through Amazon.com, retail stores, and the WalMartMovie.com website. Several days later, Robert meets with Jim, Devin, Lisa, and Sarah to make a final decision on the DVD Screamer. The possibility that the Screamer could cut into revenue-producing sales for Brave New Films and the partner organizations has become a major issue, especially when evaluated in the context of a film that will come out of the gate with a deficit of at least a half-million dollars.

It appears that the "old media" problem of exclusivity has finally reared its head. The Brave New Films team wants to get the movie and its message out by any and all means possible. Yet, in practice, there may be a very real cap on how many distribution channels can peacefully coexist. With marketing dollars in short supply, and production of the DVD Screamers as yet unfunded, adding another costly and time-intensive promotional endeavor seems like too much of a risk. The meeting ends, and the DVD Screamer is officially kiboshed, at least for this particular film.

the high cost of low price

☺ First Screening

For the last twenty-four hours, the staff has been buzzing with anticipation: The first "internal screening," originally scheduled for July 27, will take place at 4:00 p.m. on Tuesday, August 9.

The big day begins with a great piece of local press, a half-page feature story about Robert in the *Los Angeles Times* arts section. The article recaps the success of Robert's previous documentaries, and previews his upcoming project about Wal-Mart.

The second half of the article features eight paragraphs about Wal-Mart's reaction to the as-yet-unseen film and the company's broader public relations strategy in rebutting its critics. The article includes quotes from no less than three different Wal-Mart spokespeople: Sarah Clark, Nate Hurst, and Karen Burke.

Reading between the lines, both Robert and the Wal-Mart spokespeople selected their words carefully when talking to *LA Times* reporter Elaine Dutka. Neither side is willing to reveal the most sensitive aspects of their November battle plans.

In Dutka's words, Robert modestly describes his film as "the story of five people—current and former employees, as well as family business owners—affected by the policies of the retail behemoth." The actual number of interviewees is far greater, and in this interview and others Robert has steered clear of mentioning his emotional segment about crime in Wal-Mart parking lots.

Meanwhile, Wal-Mart spokesperson Hurst soft-pedals the rationale behind a November 4 academic conference that Wal-Mart suddenly announced in July. While Hurst tells the *LA Times* that the event "has been in the works for a year," Robert, Jim, and Lisa are certain that the conference is a direct response to Robert's plans, an attempt to produce company-sponsored "counterprogramming" just one week before the November 13 launch of Wal-Mart Week.

Back at the Culver City offices, the interns begin preparing for the staff screening. The screening will take place in the room that houses the high-end Avid editing system used for Robert's made-for-TV productions. The Avid system is at one end of the long room, and a thirty-six inch television is housed in a wall unit at the other end. To transform this space into a screening room, the interns are bringing in couches from other offices, aligning them facing the television like rows of church pews.

The assistant editors are frantically assembling the rough cut from the newest versions of the individual segments, some of which are still being worked on by the editors. There will not be enough time to record a videotape of the complete rough cut, so the staff screening will be enabled by a direct video feed from one of the assistant editors' Final Cut Pro edit stations.

At 3:30, the smell of popcorn begins wafting across the

courtyard. The interns are making multiple batches of microwave popcorn that will be served in red plastic cups. The off-campus staffers begin to arrive, greeting each other and wondering aloud about the movie they are about to see.

A few minutes before four, the makeshift screening room is completely packed with people. Every sofa and folding chair is full and people have staked out alternative pieces of real-estate, from the top of a video rack to the floor space underneath a desk. With twenty-five attendees, the room has become a fire marshall's nightmare.

It's a great turnout, comprising nearly everyone who has put major hours into the project. Looking around the room is like seeing a living organizational chart of the Retail Proj-

A wall-to-wall crowd at the August 9 staff screening.

ect, starting with Robert and his producers Jim Gilliam and Devin Smith. Co-producers Caty Borum, Kerry Candaele, and Sarah Feeley are here, along with principal cinematographer Kristy Tully.

Editors Doug Cheek, Chris Gordon, Jonathan Brock, and Robert Florio have settled into their seats, while assistant editors Mobolaji Olambiwonnu and Lissette Roldan put the finishing touches on the rough cut. Also in the makeshift screening room are internet researcher Meleiza Figueroa, footage researcher Jaffar Mahmood, and production coordinator Zachary Freer. Robert's political team of Lisa Smithline, Kabira Stokes, and Sharaf Mowjood have found spaces on the couch, along with comedy spot producer Laurie Levit and motion graphics specialist Bill Rude. Brave New Films partner and fund-raiser Rick Jacobs is out of town, as is co-producer Jenny Cartwright. A half-dozen interns fill in every remaining space in the now-overheated room.

Robert stands up at the back of the room and makes a brief announcement. "Thank you all for coming, and thank you for your amazing hard work. What you're about to see is a rough cut, and the sound is not yet mixed. What's helpful to us are your overall impressions of the film. A short, anonymous questionnaire will be passed out when the film ends. Please fill out your questionnaire immediately, before talking about the movie with each other."

Everybody gives Robert a warm round of applause, the lights are dimmed, and the movie starts. Just like the beginning of a typical workday at Wal-Mart, the movie commences with a big "Wal-Mart" cheer. "Give me a W! Give me an A!"

The first three minutes of the movie are filled with marching bands, singing groups, and ribbon-cuttings, intercut with the introduction of eight main characters. Sam Walton is also introduced, portrayed as the folksy founder of a great American company. Three minutes into the movie, Sam dies, and one of the former store managers explains how the company's character changed shortly thereafter.

The next hour takes the viewer on a world tour of people and communities impacted by Wal-Mart, from North Carolina, Ohio, Florida, Texas, and Colorado to London, Germany, and Quebec. Then comes the Missouri segment, a richly-painted portrait of the Esry family, who closed a four-store chain of grocery stores and are now farmers. The Esrys and their rural environment are portrayed in rich detail, while at the same time illustrating the unique tax advantages that, according to the Esrys, were only made available to Wal-Mart.

At the one hour fifteen minute mark, the crime segment begins, and there's a noticeable shift of mood in the screen-

the high cost of low price

ing room. As Laura Tanaka's story builds in intensity, so does the focus of each staff member. Filmed just one month ago, Laura's interview has become a crown jewel of the film, and everybody in the room knows it.

Another treat comes at one hour forty-five minutes, when the China segment starts. The only people in the room who are familiar with this footage are Kerry, Florio, and Robert, which makes the China segment feel shiny and new to the rest of the staff. With a wide variety of evocative B-roll, the segment tells a worker's personal story while showing the viewer places that even a seasoned world traveler would never see.

At the two-hour mark, upbeat music starts to play, and the "success stories" segment begins. Intercutting twin stories of site-fights in Inglewood, California, and Chandler, Arizona, the final segment offers the viewer hope that the Wal-Mart juggernaut can be resisted, even stopped in its tracks.

The rough cut concludes with a version of "The Star-Spangled Banner." Everyone bursts into applause at the two hour thirteen minute mark, when the credit "Directed by Robert Greenwald" appears on the screen.

By the time the lights come back on, Robert has already left the room, and the two-sided, ten-question forms are passed out along with pencils. Most of the staffers dutifully begin filling out their questionnaires, but a clot of people in the middle of the room start a noisy discussion of the film. Someone blurts out a reminder of Robert's admonition to fill out your own survey before talking to other people. Caty turns around and exclaims with a smile, "but we're a focus group!"

Caty, Kristy, Laurie, Lisa, and Chris take their "focus group" outside to the cast-iron table and chairs in the courtyard, leaving the remaining staffers to complete their forms in peace. The courtyard coffee klatch is a rapid fire exchange of passionate ideas about the strengths and weaknesses of the rough cut.

Laurie and Lisa are concerned about the opening, finding it "laborious" and "confusing" to jump between Wal-Mart's opening day festivities and brief unrelated soundbites from the main characters. Kristy misses Jonathan's "Opening Days" montage, with the pop-up counter climbing up from one to fifty.

Caty is pressing Chris on particular soundbites and shots that she feels are missing from the Middlefield and Missouri segments. Since Caty is not based in Robert's Culver City offices, this is one of her rare chances for a face-to-face sit-down with an editor, and she's making the most of it.

Everyone around the table is particularly impressed with the crime segment. Laurie calls it "an exposé" that shocks and angers the viewer. Someone wonders aloud if Robert has left the campus, but in fact he's already back at work re-cutting segments with night editor Robert Florio.

Sarah walks by, noticing that not a lot of writing is taking place amongst the group. When asked her opinion of the movie, she offers just once sentence. "Every segment can be cut by five minutes." As always, efficiency rules Sarah's personal universe.

Caty, Kristy, and Laurie decide they will forego the anonymity of the paper questionnaire and e-mail their comments to Robert instead. Getting ready to leave, Laurie tours the complex looking for Robert so that she can say congrats and goodbye. Emerging from the editor's room a minute later, Laurie announces to the courtyard staffers that "Robert needs your notes tonight! HOMEWORK!" shouts the producer-turned-full-time-mom.

Thirty-six hours later, Professor Greenwald has graded all the homework and issues a collective report card by e-mail. "Thanks to everyone for the great work, passion, and

the high cost of low price

thoughts. Just so everyone knows, the consistent comments from the screening were that people really liked China and crime, and were confused at opening. After that, for every person who wanted something cut, someone else loved or wanted more of it. That's what makes films so interesting. All your comments are going through my internal process of thought, obsession, mulling, and obsession, and I am sure the next cut will be stronger."

Robert and his editors will have six days to prepare this new rough cut, which will be shown at the "external screening" for Robert's friends and colleagues on Wednesday, August 17.

WAL*MART
the high cost of low price

Second Screening

On a beautiful, moonlit summer night, seventy of Robert's friends and colleagues have gathered in the outdoor patio of Warszawa Restaurant for the first semi-public screening of *Wal-Mart: The High Cost of Low Price*. It's an evocative, even romantic setting, with icicle lights dangling, gas heaters glowing, and a large movie screen attached to an ivy-covered brick wall.

There's a diverse group in attendance, from Robert's wife Heidi Frey and his close friend Tom Hayden to a handful of activists from local organizations that will be promoting the film. About half of the Retail Project staff is present, some of them with friends or spouses. Several of Robert's colleagues from previous film projects are having an impromptu reunion at the bar.

There's good karma for Robert in this place because the first-ever screening of *Outfoxed* was held on this very patio in the summer of 2004. Between the perfect weather, the soft tungsten light, and the feeling of being some of the first people to see something special, everyone is smiling and relaxed.

Shortly after 8:00 p.m., Robert walks to the front of the screen and gives a short welcoming speech, emphasizing the usefulness of the questionnaires that are being passed around. After thanking the owners of the restaurant, Robert motions for the film to start. Everyone claps, but the lights do not go down like in a movie theater. Apparently tonight's screening will be an alfresco, warmly-lit affair.

The movie begins in a completely different way than the version that was shown eight days ago at the staff screening. Each of the former Wal-Mart store managers introduces himself for less than a minute, and then we go right into the Middlefield segment. By the third minute we're already deep into small-town America, immersed in the Amish country of northeast Ohio.

Twenty minutes into the movie, Jonathan's "Opening Days" montage appears, complete with the recurring store opening counter graphic that appears with a "Pop-Up Video" sound effect. This particular segment hasn't been included in the film for over a month, and yet its value is obvious. In a minute or two, the huge scale and rapid growth of Wal-Mart is demonstrated in a way that offers a light moment of emotional relief after the sad story of H&H Hardware's demise.

As the movie progresses, everything feels quicker and yet richer. Dozens of new items have been added, from local news clips to informational graphics. Many of the stories pay off with a more detailed explanation of the broader context, making a case that the individual stories are the "tip of the iceberg" of Wal-Mart's corporate misbehavior.

Halfway through the screening, a cameo appearance by Wal-Mart CEO Lee Scott generates a big reaction. Introducing a segment about local communities that resist Wal-Mart's expansion plans, Scott says "When you have a group

of people, a small group of people, who don't want you in a community: Does that mean you're not going to go there?" The clip, pulled from CNBC's 2004 Wal-Mart documentary, appears a second time after two minutes of footage showing various protests and contested city council meetings from around the country. As if in response to these displays of local dissent, Scott is seen pulling his chin towards his chest and saying once again, "Does that mean you're not going to go there?" This statement triggers the biggest laughs of the evening.

There are several other audience laugh-out-loud moments, and some sniffles too. Since most of the people in the room have no familiarity at all with the footage, their reactions are a useful indicator. Listening carefully, you can hear individual viewers sigh or tsk-tsk or gasp as they encounter something particularly striking or surprising. Always working, Robert is scribbling ideas in his spiral-bound notebook, and by the time the credits roll he will have at least ten pages of comments to be discussed at tomorrow's editorial meeting.

When the movie ends, the assembled crowd gives Robert a big round of applause. Still long, this version clocks in at one hour fifty-eight minutes, a full fifteen minutes shorter than last week's version. Robert's goal is to further trim the running time down to ninety minutes, and he has two more weeks to do it.

One of Lisa's favorite colleagues, Tracy Gray-Barkham, begins discussing the movie with a friend. Tracy works at the Los Angeles Alliance for a New Economy (LAANE), the organization that spearheaded Inglewood's resistance to the Wal-Mart special election.

Tracy is excited that LAANE will be the official host of the Los Angeles premiere in early November. "It's going to be a great opportunity to mix Robert's film and television contacts with the community of local activists," she exclaims.

"There's a lot of great work being done locally, and many of the politically-active people in entertainment don't know about it."

Tracy also says that the finished DVD will be a helpful tool in explaining Wal-Mart to new people. "I actually carry information about Wal-Mart in my bag in case I need to show it to someone," she confesses, hoping that Robert's DVD can become a key addition to her persuasion arsenal.

The next day, Lisa is working the phones, looking for reactions from her activist attendees. The Reverend Peter Laarman, executive director of Progressive Christians Uniting, is brimming with ideas about how to use the film at the grassroots level. "Clearly there is an implied community that is evoked in the film of people who don't know each other," he observes. "There are lots of opportunities to connect the dots as an organizer," he says, mentioning Middlefield and Inglewood as examples of different kinds of communities who find common ground on the Wal-Mart issue.

Peter's especially intrigued by the nonpartisan tone of the film. "As an organizer, I want to figure out how to get this to show at the Unitarian Church and the Labor Hall, but also at the Rotary Club."

Always seeking to balance top-down coordination with bottom-up autonomy, Lisa asks Peter if it would be helpful for Brave New Films to offer a specific menu of different kinds of screenings and other events that grass-roots organizers could plan.

"Yes!" says Peter emphatically. People respond best with some specific action plans to choose from." Peter is upbeat about the potential of the film for religious audiences. "The moral issues raised by Wal-Mart's exploitation of everyone and everything are so obvious that they just scream for action by the religious community," he says.

Lisa's next call is to the Reverend Ron Stief of the United

the high cost of low price

Church of Christ. Ron was one of the first faith-based organizers Lisa reached out to at the beginning of the Retail Project, and he has been spreading the word for months. Lately, Ron's been working on getting mass e-mails out to various lists of politically-active church members, e-mails that ask people to sign up to host screenings on Sunday, November 13, the first day of Wal-Mart Week.

Ron explains to Lisa that the UCC has experience using videos to explore social justice issues, from water privatization to the family farm crisis. Yet in the past the UCC has produced these videos in-house, with total control over the content.

"We kind of made a leap of faith in deciding to promote a film that we hadn't yet seen, and a few people in my organization were nervous," he confesses to Lisa. "But now that I've seen it, I can honestly tell people that the film is completely compatible with our needs."

Filmmaker's Toolbox:
The Mini-Movie

During his conversation with Lisa, Reverend Ron Stief asked about the possibility of producing a twenty-minute excerpt of Robert's film, for use during church events. "You can tack on a short event before or after church, but not a long one," he explained. "People will stay an extra half-hour to watch something interesting."

According to Ron, regularly-scheduled church study groups and discussion meetings are an hour in length, too short to show a full-length feature film. "You need to create a stand-alone special event to show a full-length movie, and for this film I think there will be plenty of interest to do just that."

The Reverend Peter Laarman also asked about the availability of a twenty-minute version. "For any length event, the ideal watching-to-discussion ratio is one-to-one. So the shorter the film, the more discussion can take place before people's attention spans run out," he explained.

Requests for cut-down versions of a documentary open up a Pandora's Box of issues for a filmmaker. Is the filmmaker comfortable reducing a complex statement down to a short presentation? Should the mini-version touch on many issues, or just explore one or two? Is there time and money available to edit special versions, and, if so, what are the additional costs of distributing these versions on VHS or DVD?

One of the simplest ways to offer flexibility to organizational partners is to thoughtfully select the chapter points of your DVD. With the use of a printed or online study guide, organizations can pick and choose which chapters of the DVD to show at a time-constrained event, without any need for separate mini-versions to be produced. For the Wal-Mart movie, Main Street preservationists could watch the Middlefield and Missouri chapters, while union activists could watch a fifteen-minute segment covering the organizing struggle in Loveland, Colorado.

the high cost of low price

One of Ron's favorite characters was the Reverend Perez of Inglewood, because the film showed how she participated in leading the community resistance. "It's exciting to see clergy in specific communities reaching out and getting involved," he says. Ron signs off by telling Lisa some good news: He's getting ready to do a feature article on Robert's movie that will appear in a bimonthly newspaper that is sent to several hundred thousand churchgoers.

Reverend Altagracia Perez of Inglewood, California.

WAL★MART
the high cost of low price

😊 Time's Up

The morning after the Warszawa screening, Robert convenes an editorial department meeting that starts with a review of the looming deadlines. From the beginning of the Retail Project, the November 13 commencement of Wal-Mart Week has forced a hard stop-date on the moviemaking process. In order to have DVDs manufactured in time for the Wal-Mart Week screenings, the movie needs to be completed by October 1.

The month of September has been designated for a variety of postproduction tasks including reformatting the archival clips, working with the music composer, completing motion graphics and text overlays, mixing the sound, and color correcting the video. For a film of this complexity, four weeks is precious little time to polish and assemble the component parts, which means that the compositional process must end on Saturday, September 3.

As described in the longstanding production schedule, September 3 is the date for "picture lock," which means that every clip and every cut needs to be permanently locked in place. After picture lock, Robert's compositional process is officially over and the remaining four weeks will be devoted to technical rather than creative matters.

As the meeting starts, Robert wonders aloud if there is any way to extend the compositional process beyond September 3. "Perhaps we can break it up into reels and turn in chunks of the film rather than the whole thing," he proposes. The editorial staff discusses a variety of contingency plans that might be able to buy a few more days to finish their work. Yet the September schedule is a complex matrix of handoffs to outside vendors who will be working on individual post-production tasks, and the delay of one task can create a worrisome ripple effect.

According to Robert, the main question is "how can we use our limited time most effectively," and as soon as the meeting breaks he heads into the edit room to resume the creative process. Over the next forty-eight hours, Robert experiments with new ideas he's generated since the Warszawa screening. His goal is to test out these ideas in the first third of the movie, building a "mini rough cut" to be completed on Saturday. Upon reviewing the mini rough cut over the weekend, Robert will make a decision on whether or not the changes have improved the movie.

On Monday, August 22, the weekly editorial meeting once again begins with concern about the deadline for picture lock, which is now just twelve days away. "The biggest single mistake I made in this movie was agreeing to the deadline," laments Robert. "I did not realize that we would need five months just to find our main characters."

Before launching into a discussion about his new experiment, Robert encourages the editors to speak up when necessary. "We're trying some fairly big ideas at this juncture, so if you think I'm taking you down a road that's just

a waste of time, holler."

The biggest of these ideas involves Wal-Mart CEO Lee Scott. In mid-July, Scott declined an opportunity to be interviewed for the Retail Project. Nevertheless, in the past four days he's been upgraded from a cameo to a starring role in the film. One of Robert's takeaways from the Warszawa screening was that Lee Scott's brief soundbite in the community resistance section was a great addition. By establishing Wal-Mart's official position, the Lee Scott soundbite set up the rest of the segment as a direct rebuttal of the company line.

"I think we have a shot to make Lee Scott the anti-narrator," Robert says. "The existing cut was disorienting. One of the things I've failed to do is to let the audience know that there's a form and structure to the film." Robert explains that the problem could be remedied by applying a uniform pattern to the segments by introducing each one with a Lee Scott soundbite. Since the Retail Project has compiled archival video of several Lee Scott speeches and television interviews, there are dozens of his comments to choose from.

According to Robert, each Lee Scott soundbite would then dissolve into a map that reveals the location of the personal story to follow. The personal story thus becomes a direct response to Lee Scott's assertion about Wal-Mart's values and corporate behavior. At the end of each segment, one of Wal-Mart's own image advertisements would be contrasted with statistics about the company's actions and their impact.

"I want viewers to get into a rhythm so they can relax," Robert continues. "The statistics and Wal-Mart ads will put a button on the end of each segment, preparing us for the next Lee Scott soundbite."

After reviewing the structural changes, Robert and the editors shift to an evaluation of each individual segment. There's a free flow of ideas among the editors, who are now conversant with the entire film and offering comments on each other's work. The two recent screenings and the looming deadlines have created a common goal and brought the editorial department together as a team.

After the meeting breaks, Robert talks about his relationship with the deadlines that have governed his work for many years. "A deadline can always be met," he explains, "but the problem is the compromises that are made in order to get there." Throughout the next five days, the editorial department races to implement the "Lee Scott as anti-narrator" idea, a concept that Robert hopes will be a major improvement rather than a deadline-driven compromise.

Meanwhile, Robert's political team is also preparing for the impact of picture lock. Both Jim and Lisa have been pushing hard to complete their existing tasks, clearing the decks for a very busy fall. They both know that when Robert's compositional process is finally completed, the full power of his concentration will be turned to marketing and grass-roots organizing.

Earlier in the summer, Jim created a mini-site called Brave New Studio as a hub for anyone who wanted to get involved with the movie in a deeper way than simply hosting a screening. By mid-August, over 750 people have signed up as "field producers," and Jim and Lisa are figuring out how best to deploy them.

The first task Jim presented to the field producers was an artistic mission. Like any documentary, the Retail Project has an inexhaustible hunger for B-roll, especially shots that can be used as cutaways or as a backdrop for text. Robert has been especially interested in two particular shots of Wal-Mart locations, and it seemed both exciting and efficient to ask the field producers for help.

Robert, Jim, and Sarah decided that it would be much easier to ask the field producers to shoot digital pictures than video. Shooting professional-looking video B-roll requires

the high cost of low price

an experienced videographer, a high-quality video camera, and a tripod, which sometimes attracts unwanted attention. Snapping a quick digital picture, on the other hand, is less likely to raise the hackles of a store manager, and can be done with almost any decent digital camera.

The initial photography mission produced over one hundred photos of closed-down Wal-Mart stores, many of them very good. Jim then decided to offer up a second photo assignment, which was posted on the Brave New Studios website on August 15:

"A super low, wide angle, with lots of sky (at least 60%) photo of a Wal-Mart—AT NIGHT. The perfect shot will have a wet parking lot (after it rains) and few cars. We can dream, right? Any night shots are welcomed. This is a very last minute thing, so we need them by Wednesday, August 24th."

Motion graphics specialist Bill Rude wants this photo for a graphic he is creating for the crime segment. He's been camped out for a month in Sarah's office, building text and animations in Adobe After Effects. If one of the field producers can snap a picture that matches the request, it will help Bill make a graphic that fits in perfectly with the existing eerie B-roll being used during Laura Tanaka's wrenching story of her abduction.

On the night of August 18, field producer Tom Boese accepted the photography mission, driving south to a Wal-Mart Supercenter near Racine, Wisconsin, just hours after a severe storm had passed through the area. Boese, fifty-three years old, lives in nearby Sussex, and describes himself as a "serious amateur photographer." He became a field producer because he's concerned about small-town America and urban sprawl.

Boese e-mailed four digital images to Brave New Studios the next day, and one of the pictures was exactly what Bill Rude needed. In a strange coincidence, Boese shot his photo just a few miles from Rude's hometown in southeast Wisconsin. With only two weeks before picture lock, volunteer Tom Boese has filled an important creative need, and his evocative photo will make the final cut of *Wal-Mart: The High Cost of Low Price* (as well as the back cover of this book).

On Monday, August 29, the editorial department gathers at 9:30 a.m. for a group screening of the newest rough cut. The screening takes place in the same room where the entire staff gathered three weeks ago, but this time there are only seven people in attendance: editors Chris, Jonathan, and Florio, assistant editors Lissette and Mobolaji, footage researcher Jaffar, and a newly-hired intern. (Jaffar's recently been promoted to postproduction coordinator.)

Within days, more than half of the people in the room will already be working on other projects. Jonathan's due to wrap later this week and Mobolaji will be moving over to Robert's new Sierra Club television series on Tuesday. Florio has a new project starting on September 12, and editor Doug Cheek has already left the Retail Project, finishing his engagement on August 13 per his original agreement with Robert. The eclectic, politically-charged crew that has brought Robert a great deal of personal inspiration and satisfaction is about to disperse. "It's a unique group, among the best I have ever had," says Robert, "working endless hours for limited money."

Once picture lock has been achieved, a small team will stay on board to oversee the technical work of postproduction. Sarah will be supervising the entire process, working closely with graphics freelancer Bill Rude. Editor Chris Gordon, who has been working for Robert full-time for the last two years, will stay on board as staff editor, making last-minute changes to the film and editing trailers and DVD bonus features. Devin expects that Chris will be able to take a lengthy vacation during the last six weeks of the year, once Wal-Mart Week has passed.

Assistant editor Lissette is ready to begin the "online edit," a complicated assembly process that involves re-digitizing all of the archival clips at high-resolution and preparing the multi-track audio for export to an out-of-house audio mixer. Lissette recently had a chance to show off her own editing skills by cutting all twelve of Laurie Levit's parody ads, at least one of which seems to have found a place within the movie.

Devin expects Lissette to be the only production employee to stay on the Retail Project into next year, charged with handling requests for all sorts of customized video excerpts from the marketing team, the news media, and the many partner organizations in Lisa Smithline's growing coalition. (Lisa will be flying to Washington, DC tonight for three days of meetings with many of these partner organizations.)

The rough cut being screened today is known internally as Version 10, and is just a shade under two hours in length. Robert has asked each member of the editorial staff to take notes on the extensive changes that have been made since the Warszawa Restaurant version.

Robert joins his staffers at the conclusion of the screening to lead the editorial department's last weekly meeting. He immediately gives the floor to the staff, asking each person for comments about the newest version. Robert listens quietly as each staffer gives notes, including the new editorial intern who has only been on the project for a few weeks. The comments range from the emotional to the practical, highlighting material that is inspiring, moving, unclear, or confusing. Each of the staffers has tried to experience the newest cut as a viewer rather than a participant, and the meeting becomes a sort of focus group for Robert, using conversation rather than written questionnaires to solicit feedback.

Once everyone has had a chance to comment, Robert moves on to summarize his own concerns. "Time is now the enemy," he declares, identifying the "Opening," "Ending," and "International" sections as the ones that need the most work. Before addressing these sections, Robert wants to lock the Riverkeeper, Middlefield, and anti-union segments in the next few days so that Lissette will have some material with which to begin the online edit.

Feeling confident about Lee Scott's new role as "anti-narrator," Robert asks Jonathan to work on a new opening for the film that gives Scott a chance to lay out his own vision of Wal-Mart's place in the universe. Just as the first section of *Uncovered* featured clips of top Bush administration officials making the case for invading Iraq, the Retail Project will give the viewer a chance to absorb Wal-Mart's own corporate narrative before it is deconstructed and rebutted. In a sense, all three of Robert's documentaries are "counter-narratives" to the official images and messages of corporate and institutional power.

The meeting breaks and the editors head back to their stations. In addition to Saturday's deadline for picture lock, there's an intermediate deadline of Friday morning, when potential foreign distributors will be coming in for a screening. Robert wants the film to be in good shape for this screening, because a positive response could open up significant opportunities for overseas theatrical and home video distribution.

Tuesday is a frustrating day for Robert. There is so much creative work to do as director of the film, but the day becomes a series of meetings about legal and insurance issues. Robert drops in on the editors in between meetings, but spends most of the day cloistered in his office with Devin and a rotating cast of outside advisors.

"It's a tough job sometimes," Robert sighs. He actually has multiple jobs, directing and producing the Retail Project, executive producing two documentary television series for Brave New Films, and overseeing for-profit projects like

the high cost of low price

"Beach Girls," a miniseries that debuted on the Lifetime cable TV network this summer. Perhaps Robert is referring to his job as the main producer of *Wal-Mart: The High Cost of Low Price*, a role that requires his immersion in thorny financial and legal issues.

Shortly before 4:00 p.m., Robert watches the Riverkeeper segment one last time and declares it locked. With a running time of just five minutes, the Riverkeeper segment is one of the shortest stories in the film, but locking something, anything, is a good start. Lissette immediately begins transferring all of the Riverkeeper files to her edit station so that she can hit the ground running on the online edit.

Later in the evening, small groups of volunteer field producers will be getting together in private homes and coffee houses around the country. Back on August 17, Jim sent out an e-mail to 2,600 field producers and screening hosts, inviting them to organize local meet-ups for today, August 30. Signed by Jim, Lisa, and Kabira, the e-mail began as follows:

> *A lot of you have been asking who else and what else is happening in your area. We thought the best way to start was to give you the opportunity to meet up and get to know one another. Let each other know your thoughts and plans for your screening, promotional ideas, what your organization is doing, etc...*

By noon today, there are sixty-four meetings scheduled to take place this evening in twenty-eight states, with another half-dozen meetings planned for early September. At a minimum, this initial round of meetings will help Jim and Lisa identify the most motivated volunteers. (Field producer Tom Boese, who submitted the "wet parking lot" photo, has organized not one but two meet-ups of Retail Project supporters in southern Wisconsin.)

On Wednesday morning, Jim and Sharaf begin receiving e-mails from meet-up hosts. Jim will be sending out a questionnaire to the hosts next week, based on what he learns from the hosts who take the initiative to send in their own reports.

Shortly before 1:00 p.m., Robert locks the Middlefield segment about the demise of H&H Hardware. A few hours later, he locks one of the two sections about life as a Wal-Mart associate. With just three days to go until picture lock, Robert has now declared twenty-eight minutes of the film completed.

Thursday is a major grind, as Robert works through pages and pages of his notes trying to get the film in shape for tomorrow morning's screening. Beyond improving each segment, Robert's hoping to cut out the fat. Running time is an important consideration for the international distributors, and Robert's hoping to shave a significant chunk of time off a film that has stubbornly hovered around two hours in length. Trimming the length of the movie is also crucial for the partner organizations, so that their screenings can include a group discussion at the end of the event.

Today is editor Jonathan Brock's last day on the project. Jonathan's been Robert's flavor specialist, creating transitional sections that use multiple windows, dissolves, and graphics to convey emotion visually rather than with narrative. Instead of working on whole segments, Jonathan has created a variety of modules that plug into the segments, and all of those modules need to be finished before he leaves the project. Jonathan's also been working closely with Robert on the new opening, organizing and reorganizing dozens of Lee Scott soundbites to find the best way to let Scott tell his own story of the Wal-Mart company.

Jonathan ends up toiling at his computer until a little after midnight, tweaking the details so that he can leave the

project with a sense of closure and completion. Throughout the day, Chris and Florio are making subtle adjustments to each of the unlocked segments, getting them into good shape for tomorrow's screening. The one segment that locked today is the anti-union section, meaning that forty minutes of the film are now locked with forty-eight hours left before the deadline.

Shortly before 2:00 a.m., Mobolaji sends out an e-mail to Robert and the staff recapping the running times of the eleven segments that comprise the rough cut that the foreign distributors will view on Friday morning. At 2:30 a.m., Mobolaji heads home while the rough cut gets recorded on DVD. He's counting on the machines to work properly, as a system crash on the Macintosh G5 would torpedo the DVD dub and ruin tomorrow's screening.

Mobolaji's "set and forget" dub is completed without incident, and on Friday morning the foreign distributors come to Culver City to watch the new rough cut, internally known as Version 11. The film they see is quite a bit different from any of the previous rough cuts. It begins with excerpts from what appears to be a single Lee Scott speech at a Wal-Mart shareholders' meeting. As the stadium crowd applauds and cheers, Scott paints an upbeat picture of the company's growth, reach, and power. His comments are presented without irony or critique, setting up the rest of the film as a fair fight.

Robert's "counter-narrative" begins with Don and John Hunter of Middlefield, Ohio. The Hunters' quirky cast of long-time employees offers an unspoken contrast to the scrubbed homogeneity of Wal-Mart's own stores. As the Hunters and their employees talk about the store's long history and connections with the community, the viewer gets a feeling for what might be at stake in Wal-Mart's relentless corporate expansion.

The next thirty minutes are devoted to the inner world of

Wal-Mart, specifically the experiences of Wal-Mart's hourly associates. Version 11 is the first time that all of the employee-related material has been grouped together in one maxi-section, and the effect is powerful. Anchored by three main characters, Diane Devoy of Florida, Josh Noble of Colorado, and Edith Arana of California, the half-hour explores a con-

Former Wal-Mart associate Edith Arana.

stellation of issues raised by Wal-Mart's employment practices. In a way, this new section is a return to the "People" section Doug Cheek edited back in June, but this time it is organized around three main characters, with brief additions from a larger cast of Wal-Mart associates who chime in as needed. The "Upstairs/Downstairs" concept has been retained, as the three former Wal-Mart store managers provide insight and context on the stories told by the hourly associates.

The film then moves briskly through a series of communities that have been affected by Wal-Mart, from Missouri to the Carolinas to London, China, and Central America. In this version, Robert has saved the "Crime" section for last, offering a direct challenge to Wal-Mart's mythology that the customer always comes first. One thing that hasn't changed is the finale, an upbeat account of successful site-fights in Chandler, Arizona and Inglewood, California.

Incredibly, the version screened by the foreign distributors is fourteen minutes shorter than the rough cut the editors watched on Monday morning. The pressure of Saturday's deadline to lock picture has put the film on a crash diet, losing one eighth of its running time in just four days of work. During the foreign distributors' screening, Chris and Florio have continued cutting, and by 11:30 a.m. the third part of

WAL★MART
the high cost of low price

the Wal-Mart associates mega-section is locked. When the Missouri section locks later in the day, exactly an hour of the film will be locked, and Robert will be more than halfway towards his goal of completing the compositional process.

Lisa Smithline arrives back at the office on Friday afternoon, with lots of news about her Washington, DC trip. During the week, Lisa's spent quite a bit of time with Wal-Mart Watch, and she's impressed by the organization's rapid growth. Wal-Mart Watch now has a field staff of more than a dozen, who will be working hard this fall to organize screenings for Wal-Mart Week. Lisa leaves her final meeting with a commitment from Wal-Mart Watch to coordinate a whopping 3,500 screenings in addition to the 2,900 sign-ups that have already been generated at WalMartMovie.com. Wake-Up Wal-Mart has also committed to generate a significant number of screenings. If these goals can be accomplished, another 100,000 people will see *Wal-Mart: The High Cost of Low Price* before Thanksgiving.

According to Gina Glantz of the SEIU, the mission for the fall is activation, rather than coordination. "Everyone does not have to be aligned, just engaged," she explains. "In one community, the issue might be sprawl. In another, it might be the impact on Main Street shopkeepers. In another community, it might be a proposal to build on an historical site. Wal-Mart Week gives these groups a chance to connect their local efforts with a nationwide movement, and the film becomes a tool they can use to energize existing supporters and gain new ones."

Lisa's trip has also yielded exciting news from the office of Senator Ted Kennedy, who recently co-sponsored the Health Care Accountability Act. According to the *Washington Post*, the bill "would force states to report the names of companies that have fifty or more employees who receive government-funded health care, an effort to pressure Wal-Mart Stores, Inc.

in particular to improve employee health coverage." Kennedy is interested in showcasing his bill during Wal-Mart Week with a press conference and a high-profile Washington, DC screening.

Reviewing all the meetings and leads generated during her trip, Lisa is thrilled and also exhausted. It's time for her to go home and relax. Rather than spending Labor Day weekend slaving over an edit station trying to achieve picture lock, the political staff has three days to recharge their batteries for the marketing push ahead.

On Saturday morning, what's left of the editorial staff cranks through the remaining sections, hoping to lock as many of them as possible before tonight's deadline. After months and months of talking about it, the dreaded day of September 3 has finally arrived. Robert spends the first part of the day communicating with the editors by phone, and then comes into the office at around 4:00 p.m. to look at their work.

At the end of the day, Robert locks the "Crime," "Opening," and "Success Story" segments. He's not going to make the deadline, but he's come mighty close. The only segments that still need work are "International" (sixteen minutes), "The Walton Family Fortune," (six minutes), and a two-minute music montage that will serve as the film's conclusion. In the spirit of Labor Day, Robert gives his editors Sunday and Monday off, designating Tuesday as the final day of editing before the last three sections are locked. Although he conceals it well, Robert is utterly exhausted. He says he has never felt so mentally and physically drained.

Devin, Sarah, Lissette, and Mobolaji come in on Sunday morning to continue their efforts in the technical part of postproduction. Lissette has been rushing to keep pace with the editors, getting each segment through the online process within a day of lock. By noon, she has the entire movie in

the high cost of low price

very good shape except the three remaining sections. Robert is working from home, conducting a lengthy phone conversation with Sarah about each of the remaining graphics and animations.

Labor Day Monday is generally quiet, with only Lissette and Devin at the office. Sarah actually manages to make a trip to the beach, after some morning dialogue with Robert. Bill Rude is on his way back from a weekend trip to Taiwan to attend a friend's wedding, and Chris Gordon is enjoying his first two-day weekend in six months by visiting his family in Fresno.

On Tuesday, September 6, Robert convenes his remaining editors Chris and Florio at 8:00 a.m. sharp. Robert is extra smiley today, as if he has finally seen the light at the end of the tunnel. His marching orders for the editors are as follows: Chris will spend the day composing a new three-minute finale for the film, and Robert will be tweaking the "International" and "Walton Family" sections.

With the front edit room all to himself, Florio is rocking both edit bays today, using his own system for the "International" segment and Jonathan's system for the "Walton Family" segment. Since Doug Cheek's mid-August departure, Florio has been tweaking and restructuring all of Doug's segments, and now that Jonathan has left, Florio is also putting finishing touches on those segments as well. By the time that picture lock has been achieved, Florio's hand will have touched more than one hour of the film. Not bad for the "night editor," who was the fourth and last editor brought on to the project.

Meanwhile, Chris is spending the morning in "compositional mode," trying to create a symphony from the "cacophony" of community resistance clips that are available to him. Robert drops in and explains that he wants the ending to be "uplifting and energizing, but not *The Sound of Music.*

We have to balance the celebration of victories with the on-going threat posed by Wal-Mart's expansion."

Jotting down a note on Robert's feedback, Chris realizes his pen has run out of ink. "That's weird…" he tells Robert, "this is the pen I've been using since the very start of the project." Perhaps the planets are aligning for picture lock to be achieved tonight.

In late afternoon, Robert locks the "International" section. Now there are only two segments remaining: the six-minute "Walton Family" segment and a three-minute montage of community resistance at the very end of the film. Over the last four days, the running time of the movie has shrunk by one minute.

As the sun sets, Lissette starts onlining the "International" segment. Florio is digging into the "Walton Family" section, and Chris is working furiously on the finale. Robert jokes with Sarah about "bringing in blankets and mattresses" for a long night ahead.

Just a few hours later, the road to picture lock takes a sharp left turn. Robert visits Chris at around 9:30 p.m. to look at the latest version of the finale, and decides that it's not ready for prime time. Rather than polishing an existing segment, Chris is trying to create one from scratch, and a single day, even a long day, just isn't enough time.

Robert makes a snap decision to send Chris home and delay picture lock for eighteen hours. Lissette and Sarah are still eager to get as close to complete lock as possible, and so Robert refocuses on completing the "Walton Family" segment tonight. Yet one hour later, at 10:30 p.m., Robert also sends Florio home. There's no reason to rush the completion of Florio's segment if Chris is getting one more day to finish the finale.

The next morning, Chris and Florio hone their sections while Robert moves on to the next stage of postproduction.

Now that the bulk of the film is locked, the composer and music supervisor can hone in on the music cues, and they have come to Culver City for a spotting session. Instead of locking picture in a late-night blaze of glory, Robert locks the remaining two segments during brief visits to the edit bay while taking breaks from the music spotting session. There's no popping of corks, and minimal celebration, because a mountain of technical work still needs to be done in order to complete the film by October 1.

At the end of the day, Robert takes a moment to reflect on the completion of his compositional process. Throughout the spring and summer, the Retail Project has grown in scale and complexity, and completing it has become a bigger task than Robert ever envisioned. The Wal-Mart megacorporation has proved to be a fertile subject, and will be a formidable adversary in the fall. As he leaves the office to head home, Robert shares a thought with the staff about his nearly-completed documentary. "On a commercial film, the only judge is success at the box office," he says, "but here the pressure is much higher. The ultimate judge of our work is whether this film can inspire people to make change."

WAL-MART
the high cost of low price

RESOURCES FOR FURTHER READING

Official Sites Relating to *Wal-Mart: The High Cost of Low Price:*
www.WalMartMovie.com
www.BraveNewFilms.org
www.RobertGreenwald.org

The Author's Sites:
www.GregSpotts.com
www.AmericanJobsFilm.com

Wal-Mart Official Sites:
www.WalMart.com
www.WalMartStores.com
www.WalMartFacts.com

Union-Backed Sites Critical of Wal-Mart:
www.WalMartWatch.com
www.WakeUpWalMart.com

Advocacy for Small Town Main Streets:
www.sprawl-busters.com

The *Dukes v. Wal-Mart Stores, Inc.* Gender Discrimination Lawsuit:
www.WalMartClass.com

Wal-Mart's Relationships With Suppliers:
www.fastcompany.com/magazine/77/walmart.html

Wal-Mart Child-Labor Settlement With US Labor Dept:
www.edworkforce.house.gov/democrats/walmartqanda.html

Wal-Mart Illegal Immigration Settlement With US Immigration and Customs:
www.cbsnews.com/stories/2005/03/18/national/
main681593.shtml

Conditions in Overseas Factories Producing Goods for Wal-Mart:
www.nlcnet.org/news/whistleblower.asp

2004 Academic Conference on Wal-Mart: Program of Speakers and Downloadable Papers
www.ihc.ucsb.edu/walmart/schedule.html

Acknowledgements

First and foremost, I am deeply thankful to Robert Greenwald and my publisher Gary Baddeley for inviting me along on a wonderful journey. Robert and Gary conceived of this book in the spring of 2005 and began looking for a writer. Gary's right-hand-man Ralph Bernardo recommended me as a candidate, and I visited Robert's Culver City offices on April 18 for an interview.

Writing this book has been a challenge. I was hired in early May and the book was due on Labor Day. Sometimes I felt like a blogger rather than an author, writing about events in real time rather than having the luxury of reflecting on what I had just witnessed.

Robert and his entire staff were always welcoming and helpful, even while under intense pressure to complete their own assignments. Everyone quickly thought of the book as another important part of Robert's multifaceted project, and provided me with unlimited information and access.

Having directed a self-funded documentary film the previous year, I found it fascinating to observe documentary filmmaking on a much larger scale. Although few documentarians can marshal resources on the scale of Robert Greenwald, I believe there are many tools and techniques used on the Retail Project that can be adapted for any size project.

As always, my family has been a tremendous source of support and comfort. My father Jules Spotts and college buddies Kari Steeves and Blake Koh supplied valuable feedback on early versions of the manuscript, and my attorney Robert Solomon helped me to better understand the publishing business. UCSB professor Nelson Lichtenstein's academic conference on Wal-Mart was my first exposure to many of the issues explored in this book, and I am sure many other participants also look back at that conference as an enlightening event. Disinformation staffers Jason Louv and Maya Shmuter worked long hours on copyediting and layout in order to meet our deadline.

Finally, I'd like to thank everyone who agreed to appear in front of Robert's cameras. Following the film-in-progress, I was exposed to many more stories than those that made the final cut, and was moved by each and every one of them.

WAL-MART
the high cost of low price

About the Author

Greg Spotts is an author and filmmaker based in Southern California. This book is his third consecutive project exploring the changing global economy and its impact on American workers. In January of 2004, Spotts quit his job producing televised concerts and soccer matches to travel around the country interviewing Americans who had recently lost their jobs due to low-wage foreign competition. The resulting film, *American Jobs*, was self-released on DVD on Labor Day 2004 and has since been featured on CNN, PBS, NPR, Sirius, XM Satellite Radio and many other national and local media outlets.

When the Disinformation Company acquired distribution rights to *American Jobs* in late 2004, Spotts decided to write a companion book for the film. In February 2005, Disinformation published his book, *CAFTA and Free Trade: What Every American Should Know*. The book was widely circulated in Washington, DC as a lobbying tool during the congressional debate over the Central American Free Trade Agreement, and was lauded by US Representative Hilda Solis in a speech on the House floor.

Originally focused on a career managing talent in the music business, Spotts co-founded the Shortlist Music Prize in 2001 and executive produced Shortlist concert specials for MTV Networks in 2003 and 2004. Also in 2003, Spotts produced the opening day festivities for the $140 million Home Depot Center soccer stadium, and served as Supervising Producer of Television and Stadium Entertainment for the Los Angeles Galaxy soccer team.

Spotts publishes a blog at **www.gregspotts.com**.

Also from disinformation® and Greg Spotts:

American Jobs
DVD * $14.95 (US) * 826262001094
Disturbed by the news that three million manufacturing jobs
had disappeared between 2000 and 2003, Greg Spotts hit the
road with a video camera to see the damage for himself.

CAFTA and Free Trade: What Every American Should Know
Trade Paperback * 96 pages * ISBN: 1-932857-16-8 * $7.95 (US)
Applies a critical lens to the recently-signed Central American
Free Trade Agreement and reveals broader truths about Amer-
ica's risky position in the new global economy.

Also from disinformation® and Robert Greenwald:

Wal-Mart: The High Cost of Low Price
DVD * $12.95 (US) * 826262001896

The Robert Greenwald Documentary Collection
4 DVD Set * $29.95 (US) * 826262001391
Uncovered chronicles the Bush Administration's determined
quest to invade Iraq following the events of September 11, 2001.
Outfoxed examines how media empires, led by Rupert Murdoch's Fox News, have been running a "race to the bottom" in
television news.
Unconstitutional explores how the Patriot Act has taken away
checks on law enforcement and continues to endanger the civil
liberties of all Americans.
The **Bonus Disc** contains a special address to owners of the
Documentary Collection from Robert Greenwald in which he
explains the genesis of each of the films.
All films also available individually for $9.95 (US).